Graduate School

Winning Strategies for Getting In
With or Without Excellent Grades

Dave G. Mumby, Ph.D

PROTO PRESS

Graduate School
Winning Strategies For Getting In With or Without Excellent Grades

By Dave G. Mumby, Ph.D

Published by:

Proto Press Publications
Post Office Box 818
Hudson, Quebec
Canada J0P 1H0
www.mygraduateschool.com

Printed in Canada by Transcontinental Métrolitho

10 9 8 7 6 5 4 3

Canadian Cataloguing In Publication Data

Mumby, David Gerald, 1962-
        Graduate school: winning strategies for getting in with or without excellent grades

Includes index.
ISBN 0-9682173-4-6   ISBN13 978-09682173-4-4

        1.Universities and colleges—Canada—Graduate work—Admission. 2. Universities and colleges—United States—Graduate work—Admission. I. Title.

LB2371M85   378.1'6'0971   C97-900512-4

TABLE OF CONTENTS

II. HOW TO PREPARE A WINNING APPLICATION

III. GOING BEYOND THE REQUIREMENTS

Acknowledgements

I first wish to acknowledge the contributions of the many people who influenced my thinking, either directly or indirectly, as I wrote this book. Some of them are Graduate Program Directors, Deans, Department Heads, and other faculty members from various departments and schools who were generous enough to put aside time in their busy schedules to meet with me to discuss graduate studies in their areas. These people include: Twareque Ali, John Capobianco, Andrew Dutkewych, Greg Garvey, James Gavin, Bob Kavanaugh, Martin Kusy, Patsy Lightbown, Reeta Tremblay, and Norman White. I also wish to thank the many friends and colleagues who were kind enough to serve as peer-reviewers of the unfinished manuscript. Each of them offered many useful suggestions that contributed to an improved manuscript. These people include: Shirley Black, Colin Ellard, Eric Hargreaves, Alicia Hunt, Nadine Jeffries, Syd Miller, Jim Pfaus, John Pinel, Michael von Grunau, Norman White, and Jodye Yates. Muriel Conant has my deepest gratitude for her generous donation of time to proofreading and editing the complete manuscript. One person made a notably substantial and invaluable contribution — Susan Hawke, Associate Librarian at the Career Resource Centre of Concordia University, single-handedly compiled the annotated listings of reference materials in the *Resources* section. And finally, I owe a special debt to Charles H.M. Beck, my first academic mentor. His advice and support enabled me to get into graduate school many years ago, and without the faith that he had in my abilities, the rest of my academic career, and this book, would not have happenned.

Disclaimer

This book is designed to provide information concerning the subject matter covered. Its purpose is not to reprint all of the information that is otherwise available to the author and/or publisher, but rather to complement, clarify, and supplement the material in other texts. For more information, see the many references listed in the *Resources* section near the back of this book.

The book deals with topics on which opinions may vary. It offers advice that reflects the opinions of the author, and it should not be expected that all other individuals within the academic community will agree, entirely and unconditionally, with all of the ideas that are expressed. The author shall have neither liability nor responsibility to any person who fails to get into graduate school after reading this book.

Chapter 1

How to Use this Book

Many students have serious misconceptions about what graduate school involves and about what it takes to be accepted into a graduate program. Every year, countless students apply to graduate school but fail to get in because they make fatal mistakes during the application process. This happens frequently, even to students with excellent grades. In most cases, they are unaware that they are doing anything wrong, and they make these mistakes because they are more or less in the dark about how the process of selecting applicants really works. Most of their mistakes could easily be avoided, if only they had a better idea of what they should be doing.

Meanwhile, many of the same misconceptions prevent thousands of other qualified students from giving much thought to graduate or professional school. Many of these students mistakenly believe that they don't have a realistic chance of getting in, and often, it is because they think that their grades are not good enough. But the truth is that most of them *do* have a good chance. They are simply unaware of the many ways that one can overcome mediocre grades and still get into graduate school.

This book explains what applicants to graduate or professional schools should be doing, what they shouldn't be doing, and why.

Most readers of this book are presumed to be undergraduate college or university students who are either currently planning to apply to graduate or professional school, or who have not yet made that decision but eventually will. There is an excellent chance that you will be accepted and eventually obtain an advanced degree, such as a master's, a doctorate, or a professional degree. When the day eventually comes that you find yourself enjoying a comfortable lifestyle and a fine career, I hope that you will think back on this book as having helped you get there.

This book is aimed at two kinds of student: *The first kind of student has average to above-average grades — grades that are respectable, but that would not be considered excellent or outstanding.* For students of most disciplines, I am speaking, generally, of grade-point-averages (GPAs) in the B-minus to B-plus range. Most of these students would not be accepted into graduate school unless they did some things to overcome the shortcomings in their grades. One way to deal with a mediocre GPA is to study harder and more effectively. But, the purpose of this book is not to help with that. Instead, it explains how students with average to above-average grades can improve their chances of getting into graduate school *despite* their grades.

The second kind of student that this book is meant for has very good or excellent grades. For students of most disciplines this would mean a GPA of A-minus or better. Many such students mistakenly think that good grades are all that is needed to get into graduate school. It is sad and unfortunate, although not uncommon, for students to work hard to achieve excellent grades only to make errors of judgment later on when applying to graduate school and fail to get in altogether. Many of them have assumed for a long time that they would eventually go to graduate school and earn an advanced degree. What a bitter disappointment it is when they are rejected by every program they apply to, and they begin to realize that the career they have longed for and worked so hard for might just be an impossible dream.

The cruelest irony is that many A-plus students are rejected for admission into graduate programs while other students are accepted into the same programs with grades that are more like Bs!

You don't think you can get into graduate school with Bs? In fact, thousands of students across North America do it every year. I did. My undergraduate GPA was somewhere around a B when I applied to graduate school. I was accepted into a program, eventually earned my master's and doctoral degrees, and now enjoy a successful and rewarding career. This sort of thing happens often, and there is probably no reason why it can't happen to you, if you are willing to take the necessary steps. This book will show you how.

> *There are a variety of grading scales used in North American colleges (e.g., A - F letter grades, percentage scale, 0.0 - 4.0 scale, and more). The letter-grade scale is used throughout this book for the sake of simplicity.*

This book dispels some common myths about what is required for successful application to graduate school, particularly those myths concerning the necessity of exceptionally high grades. It examines how the process of selecting graduate-school applicants really works (in most cases), and what important factors exist beyond grades that determine the success or failure of an application. It outlines strategies that students can begin using immediately to improve their chances of getting into graduate school and earning an advanced degree. Much of the information and advice in this book is aimed primarily at undergraduates, but most of it will also be useful to students who are currently in master's programs and who expect to eventually apply to a doctoral program.

Of course, I cannot guarantee that you will get into graduate school just by reading this book. But I can guarantee you this: **If you understand the advice in this book, and use good judgment in how you apply it to your own situation, you will greatly improve your chances of being accepted into graduate school.** In the end, *you* will be the one who determines whether you succeed — but I know some ways that you can help yourself.

Most of the ideas and suggestions in this book apply to the vast majority of programs, departments, faculties, and schools in the United States and Canada. But it is vitally important to realize that not all of the information, opinions, and suggestions will apply in all instances. There are substantial differences among graduate programs, even within a particular field. Not surprisingly, the differences *across* fields are even greater. Some of the ideas that we discuss may be irrelevant to students in certain disciplines. You will need to be flexible and adapt your specific actions to situations as they arise.

There are some special issues that are relevant to certain groups of students, but that are not dealt with in this book. For instance, someone who earned an undergraduate degree years ago and who now wants to go to graduate school after having been in the work force for several years will probably encounter situations that are not discussed in this book. Neither does this book discuss some of the issues that face members of visible minority groups, or international students, or students with disabilities. Increasingly, students are entering graduate programs in areas different from those in which they concentrated as undergraduates. Students who do this may occasionally encounter unique situations that are not considered in this book. There are books that deal with some of these special issues listed in the *Resources* section (Special category guides) near the back of this book.

> *Although there are significant differences between graduate and professional schools, this book deals mainly with features that are common to both kinds of advanced-degree program. The terms "graduate school," "graduate program," and "graduate studies," are generally favored throughout this book for stylistic reasons only. Accordingly, readers who are interested in professional school should assume that much of the information and advice contained herein applies equally to their objectives.*

This book is not intended to be the sole resource for any student who is applying to graduate or professional school. Rather, its purpose is to acquaint students in most disciplines with the kinds of things they should know and expect to encounter when applying to almost any advanced-degree program. For the most part, therefore, this book is concerned with *commonalities* that exist across most graduate programs, in most fields. There are a few good books and other publications that offer more specific information and advice to students in certain fields but, unfortunately, the list is not long. Aside from professional programs in business, law, and medicine, not many fields are covered. Begin your search for the answers you need by reading this book, and follow up later with a trip to the library or a visit to a career counsellor to find out whether there are other advisement books aimed specifically at students in your field of study. Several are listed in the *Resources* section at the back of this book.

How the Book is Organized

This book has three main sections: The first section, **Truths & Myths About Graduate School**, explains why some of the widely held ideas that students have about graduate school are inaccurate. This section explains why graduate school can be a more attractive option than many people realize; I hope it will motivate students to seriously consider it. Chapter 2 gives hope to students who feel unqualified to gain entry into a graduate program because their grades are less than outstanding. Meanwhile, this chapter should also instil a little bit of healthy caution into students who believe that their outstanding grades will virtually guarantee that they get into graduate school.

You need to understand what graduate study in your discipline is all about before you can plan an effective strategy for getting into the right graduate program and for having success once you are there. Chapter 3 covers some of the things that you need to know before you can plan a successful application. For instance, in order to devise a successful plan, you need to understand the process by which applicants are selected in most programs. **Most of the mistakes that students make when applying to graduate school stem from not understanding how or why the successful applicants are selected, or why the unsuccessful ones are rejected.** Chapter 3 describes some of the common selection processes. This chapter also describes the basic components of most graduate school applications and the roles that each of them play in leading to the success or failure of an applicant.

Your success will also depend on choosing a graduate program that is suited to your specific goals, and in those disciplines where graduate studies are done under the supervision of a faculty member, on the selection of an appropriate supervisor. Chapter 4 offers suggestions on how to make these important decisions.

The second section, **How To Prepare an Application That Will Beat the Competition,** will get you started on improving your chances of getting into a graduate program. Chapter 5 clarifies the nature of the competition involved in applying to graduate school. This understanding will enable you to prepare a general strategy for gaining an advantage over other applicants. Chapters 6 and 7 explain what admissions committees and faculty members are really looking for when they assess the various components of your application. These two chapters are full of suggestions to help you enhance each component of your application, making it stand out and above the rest of the crowd.

The third section, **Going Beyond the Requirements,** is all about taking *extra* steps that will greatly improve your chances of being accepted into a graduate program. Most of the ideas and strategies outlined in chapters 8 and 9 never even occur to most students, but those who do use them are almost always successful.

To help you plot and execute an effective strategy, an idealized *plan and timetable* is outlined in chapter 10. Keep in mind that not all aspects of this plan will be appropriate for applying to all programs. Moreover, many of the steps that are suggested are best to take at a certain point in time before applying to graduate school. Remember, this is just an *idealized* plan. Not all of the steps are applicable to all types of programs, and depending on how much time you have before you graduate, there will be compromises and improvisations that you will need to make in accordance with your own situation.

The final section, **Resources,** contains lists of books, guides, and directories, which students will find extremely valuable as they prepare for application to graduate or professional school. Full reference information is provided for all of these resources. Some are mentioned occasionally throughout the book, in places where they seem particularly relevant.

I strongly recommend that you first read this entire book so that you can combine all of the information and recommendations into a good overall strategy. Then as you go through the application process you will want to refer back to particular sections, so keep it handy.

Where the Advice Comes From

The information, opinions, and advice in this book came from four main sources: One was my own observations and experiences as a faculty member, a graduate supervisor, and as a member of graduate admissions committees (the nature and the role of admissions committees are described in Chapter 3). Many of the opinions in this book reflect the way that I personally evaluate graduate-school applicants — the positive and negative indicators that I look for. It should be noted that my method is not unique; most of my colleagues generally approach the task of evaluating applicants the same way I do.

The second main source of opinion and advice was from interviews that I conducted with Graduate Program Directors in various departments and faculties, and from informal discussions with faculty members in various departments at other universities. These people are experts, and they offered dozens of tips on how students can improve their chances of getting into graduate school. The findings of these interviews, surveys, and frank discussions are reflected in the advice given throughout this book.

The third main source of information for this book was other advisement books that deal with specific aspects of applying to graduate school, or applying to graduate school in particular fields. Complete reference information for many of them can be found in the *Resources* section.

Some of the advice also comes from my own experiences and observations as a student. I have been through the process of applying to graduate school and getting in, despite having a mediocre undergraduate GPA. And I have seen dozens of other students do the same thing. It amazes me how pervasive are the common misconceptions and misunderstandings that most students have concerning graduate studies and how to get into graduate school. Most of the students that I meet on campus today have the same mistaken ideas about graduate school that I shared with my peers many years ago.

Get Started Now!

Something that I hate having to do as part of my job is denying certain students entrance into our graduate programs. Many wishful applicants are rejected each year. I often consider that many of these rejected students are probably well-suited for graduate school but may never find out because their applications were unable to convince me that they truly have what it takes. I feel sorry for these students, but there is nothing I can do about their inability to sell themselves.

Occasionally, one comes across applicants who do an exceptional job of demonstrating that they possess attributes necessary for success in graduate school and in a related career afterwards. Those are the applicants who are accepted. You should be one of those applicants, and there is no reason why you can't be if you are willing to make appropriate use of the information and advice in this book.

Whether you are in your freshman or senior year, the time to begin planning for your graduate-school application is now. Don't wait until you are in your final semester of your senior year to begin taking the steps outlined in this book. Some of the recommended steps take a good deal of time to implement. The longer you wait, the more difficult it will be to improve your chances of getting into graduate school. Conversely, the sooner you begin, the easier it will be. But don't panic if you discover that you do not have enough time to take advantage of all of the strategies described in this book. There are a great many things that you can do "at the last minute" to improve your chances.

If you have weak grades and no notable and relevant accomplishments, then you might decide after reading this book that you don't have a realistic chance of getting into graduate school this year no matter what you do. Consider it a blessing that you figured this out before you wasting time and money, and experiencing much anguish. If you are serious about getting into graduate school, then you have plenty of time to take advantage of the advice in this book and prepare for application next year.

TYPES OF PROFESSIONAL SCHOOLS

Graduate training in fields other than the humanities and sciences is generally designed for particular occupations. Although there is no clear agreement on how to demarcate areas of professional study, the following nineteen disciplines are the dominant ones: architecture, business, dentistry, education, engineering, forestry, journalism, law, library science, medicine, nursing, optometry, pharmacy, physical therapy, public health, social work, theology, and veterinary medicine.

I. Truths & Myths About Graduate School

Each year, thousands of students with excellent grades apply to graduate school or professional school and fail to get in. Contrary to what you might expect, it is *not* because they are beaten out by other applicants with *even better* grades. They fail to get in because they make mistakes in the application process. These mistakes often stem from common misconceptions about graduate school.

Meanwhile, many students doubt they will ever have a master's or doctoral degree because they think that their grades are not good enough to get into graduate school or professional school. Most of them are wrong. In fact, most have a good chance of getting into a graduate program and earning an advanced degree — if they take the right steps. The problem is they don't know the actual criteria used to select who gets in.

The next few chapters will set the record straight on what graduate study is all about, and what it takes to get into graduate or professional school and to earn an advanced degree.

Life is full of choices, and some of the choices we make will have profound affects on our futures. One such choice could be graduate or professional school. Is it the best way for you to get from where you are to where you want to be? To know the answer, you must first understand what graduate school is. As you learn more about graduate school, you will probably be pleasantly surprised to discover that it has more rewards than you had previously imagined!

Chapter 2

Why More Students Should Consider Graduate School

Grad school? Me? Are You Kidding?

You hear the same thing time after time. If you ask undergraduate university or college students whether they plan to go to graduate school and earn an advanced degree (e.g., master's, doctorate), they often often reply with something like,

> "I'd like to, but I can't afford to spend another five or more years in school. I value my education, but I don't find what I'm studying so interesting that I would want to delve into it any deeper. I just want to get my bachelor's degree and get a job. Besides, my grades aren't good enough to get into grad school."

This kind of response is typical. Unfortunately, it also reflects some of the most common misconceptions and misunderstandings about graduate school.

Consider the first part of the response — the part about not being able to afford to stay in school. Many students have the misconception that going to graduate school would mean struggling to make financial ends meet the same way that they did when they were undergraduates. It is true that in some cases there can be considerable expense associated with years of graduate study. But, the truth is also that there are many more ways to finance graduate school than undergraduate school. This topic is discussed in more detail in Chapter 3.

For now, the important thing for you to realize is that most graduate students are able to maintain a good income while working toward an advanced degree. In fact, most graduate students are *paid* to go to school! The money may be a stipend from a bursary, scholarship, or fellowship, or salary for teaching assistantships or research assistantships, or even a straightforward salary arrangement in which the graduate student receives a stipend from the graduate supervisor's research or teaching grants.

> *A specific example provides some perspective on the kinds of financial support that are sometimes in place for graduate students: The department that I work in guarantees a minimum level of support of $10,000 per year for graduate students (as of 1996-97). That is a minimum — guaranteed. Most of the graduate students in our department are making closer to $14,000, and some even more. Most of the money is from the supervisor's research grants, but many students also earn a few thousand dollars per year for working as teaching assistants. Meanwhile, they receive the training that will eventually put them into the competition for some of the best jobs in their field.*

Financial hardship may be a typical part of being an undergraduate, but it is less common for a graduate student. A typical graduate student's income will not lead to great riches, but it is usually enough to pay tuition and living expenses (rent, groceries, a trip home during Christmas holidays, etc.). And that sure beats having to take out a student loan or work at a part-time job in order to get by while you further your education. Many graduate students don't have to look for a summer job every year because they are "employed" all year round. Not all graduate students are able to avoid taking a loan, but many can and do get by without it.

There are other financial benefits available to graduate students: If you owe money for student loans that you took out while you were an undergraduate, then enroling in full-time graduate studies may allow you to continue to defer repayment of those loans. Most student loans maintain some kind of interest-relief until the student is entirely finished with full-time study. And as already mentioned, you probably won't need to take out any more loans in order to survive while you are a graduate student. Of course, your advanced degree can help place you into a high-paying career that will make it easier to pay back your previous loans.

Now consider the second part of the typical student's response which began this chapter — the part about not being sufficiently interested in one's undergraduate specialization or major to want to pursue graduate studies. The truth is that graduate school is more rewarding than many people think. Most students find graduate studies to be infinitely more interesting than undergraduate studies. Few undergraduates understand what really happens in graduate school, because no one ever explains it to them.

A common misconception about graduate school is that there is considerable focus on taking classes where you delve deeply into a narrow range of subject matter in order to become an expert or specialist. In fact, course work and in-class testing are relatively minor parts of many graduate programs, especially beyond the masters level. Instead, research and skills development are usually the focus, especially once you are past the master's level. You will be too busy learning *useful* things in graduate school to sit in a classroom for hours each day.

Most undergraduate degree programs are aimed at providing students with a broad understanding of a discipline and the career options that are available within that particular field, but some of them do relatively little to actually train you for a great career. Graduate programs, on the other hand, are aimed at training and developing independent specialists, researchers, scholars, professionals, etc.

Now getting back to our analysis of the typical student's response to the question of whether he or she plans to go to graduate school, consider the part about wanting to finally get out of school and get a job. Well, as we have already discussed, most graduate students earn an income while they work on their master's or doctorate.

In other words, being a graduate student *is* a job! You could think of it as a temporary job — one that lasts a few years.

Going to graduate school is like having a job, but in and of itself graduate studies is certainly not a career. But, neither are many of the jobs that students end up with after obtaining their undergraduate degrees and looking for work. In fact, in today's job market, some people manage to earn a better living by *staying* in school and working on an advanced degree than by finishing with the same run-of-the-mill undergraduate degree as everyone else and finding themselves either unemployed or with only a temporary or second-rate job. An undergraduate degree gives most people a modest job-market advantage over the typical high-school graduate, but an advanced degree gives most people a huge advantage over those with only an undergraduate degree.

> *For most people, the greatest and most lasting reward that comes from obtaining an advanced degree is not the sense of accomplishment or prestige, but rather the opportunity to do work that holds intrinsic interest for them. For those who obtain professional degrees, it may also be the wide range of exciting career options and the earning power. Some graduate students already have careers, and they wish to upgrade their credentials to facilitate advancement in those careers, or to obtain a wider range of career options.*

Why would anyone want to end their formal education with an undergraduate degree when they were within reach of an advanced degree and all of its rewards? It may be true that an advanced degree is not realistically within reach of every student, but it is within reach of tens of thousands of students who mistakenly think that they are not even qualified to try. Graduate school might not be the right choice for everyone, but you owe it to yourself to at least give it some consideration.

You May Be More Qualified Than You Think

Every year, thousands of students apply to graduate schools in North America. Most of them apply to more than one school, and those who are serious in their desire to get into graduate school are eventually accepted into a program, somewhere. For many, the decision to go to graduate school and obtain an advanced degree has been part of their education and career plans since they first entered college or university. For those individuals, the advanced degree is an absolute prerequisite for their career goals. For others, the decision to go to graduate school came only after they had been in college or university for a few years and began to question how valuable their undergraduate degree would be when they finally entered the job market.

Why grades aren't always the most important factor   Now consider the greatest of the common misconceptions about graduate school — the idea that you must have outstanding undergraduate grades to get into graduate school and to succeed once you are there. Do you believe this? I suspect that you probably do...because most students believe it, and because I used to believe it, too.

But it's simply not true! Although outstanding grades certainly help your chances of getting into graduate school, there are ways to get in even if you do not have excellent grades. This book will show you how.

Have you ever been told or have you thought to yourself that you haven't got a hope of ever going to graduate school because you are not an Honors student? That's complete nonsense! I know dozens of Ph.Ds who were never Honors students. I have three degrees: a B.Sc., M.Sc., and a Ph.D, and was never an Honors student.

But what if you have only average or slightly above-average grades? Could you really expect to succeed in graduate school with grades like that? Absolutely! Once you begin your graduate studies, you are just as likely to obtain a master's or doctoral degree as many of your current classmates who get As and A-pluses in all of their classes.

It might be hard to believe that this is true, but it is. It has to do with the ways that students are taught and evaluated in graduate school. The methods of learning and evaluation are so different from those of undergraduate school that some students' undergraduate GPA can be a rather poor predictor of their future performance in graduate school.

Although there have been studies that found significant correlations between undergraduate GPA and graduate school success in some disciplines, these analyses typically involved very large groups of students, and many graduate-program faculty members would argue that the correlation is not so apparent when considering only the students in their own program. Even in disciplines in which there are thought to be stronger relations between undergraduate grades and graduate school success, no one would deny that there are frequent exceptions, and almost any graduate-program faculty member knows of cases in which students with suspect undergraduate grades turned out to be among the best graduate students.

> *Students who get into graduate school and do their best to fulfil the requirements will usually obtain at least one advanced degree, either a master's or a doctorate. Similarly, most students who are accepted into a professional-degree program, and who put in a reasonable effort while they are there, will eventually obtain the degree they are after.*

There are graduate programs in which applicants are rejected more or less automatically if their grades are below some ridiculously high minimum. Obviously, you would need higher grades to get into one of the most competitive programs in North America than to get into one of the hundreds of less competitive programs. But as you will soon discover, in the majority of schools and disciplines, the acceptance and rejection of graduate-school applicants is far from being an automatic process based entirely on grades.

Before we go any further, it's important that we clarify something: Although I have been emphasizing that students can get into graduate school without an outstanding undergraduate GPA, it definitely *is* true that in most graduate programs, the quality of undergraduate grades is an important criterion for evaluating applicants. What many students fail to realize, however, is that this is only *one* of the important criteria, and that a shortcoming in terms of undergraduate

GPA can often be compensated for by excellent performance on some of the other important criteria.

It is equally important to emphasize here what I mean when referring to grades that are not outstanding, but still good enough to get into graduate school: In most areas of study, this includes students with a GPA between B-minus and B-plus. Very few programs in any discipline would accept applicants with a GPA lower than B-minus, no matter what other strengths such an applicant possessed, although there may be rare exceptions in some disciplines.

The relative importance of undergraduate grades varies widely across programs within a particular field, depending on the prestige or competitiveness of the program. Not surprisingly, the differences *across* disciplines are even greater.

Some programs have minimum entry requirements with respect to undergraduate GPA, but these are usually not very high, and few applicants are weeded out because their grades are too low. Moreover, these minimum-requirement rules are not always written in stone, and you can sometimes get around them if you know what to do. More on this later.

> *It is easy to see why students would mistakenly assume that admission to graduate school depends mainly on obtaining or surpassing some minimum grade-point requirement. After all, that is the main qualification for admission to many undergraduate programs. Without ever being told otherwise, why wouldn't a student assume that the same is true for graduate school admission?*

A special message to students with excellent grades   Even if you have an outstanding GPA and the highest grades in your graduating class, you cannot afford to be complacent or overconfident in your approach to graduate school application. Your outstanding grades are no guarantee that you will be accepted into the graduate program of your choice...or even into any graduate program at all!

Many students with top grades fail to get into graduate school because they have no idea what they are doing when they apply. They don't really understand what graduate admissions committees are looking for in an applicant, so they unwittingly sabotage their own chances by revealing their naivete or by not dealing properly with certain parts of the application.

By the time you are finished reading this book, you will understand why you need more than your good grades in order to get into the graduate program you want. As you will see, it comes down to this: Graduate program admissions committees aim to accept the best *people*, not necessarily the best credentials.

Do you need to be in an Honors program?   First, you need to understand that there are at least two different ways that the term "Honors" is used in undergraduate programs. The first way, which is also the most common usage, is simply as a designation which recognizes that a particular student has an outstanding GPA. Outstanding undergraduate grades are more important when applying to graduate school in some fields than in others, and most master's programs in these fields will insist that an applicant has achieved undergraduate Honors. But even though undergraduate Honors may be listed as a program requirement, this doesn't always mean that you can't get into these programs without an Honors GPA. A GPA that is less than outstanding will often be adequate if you can demonstrate that your grades do not fairly reflect your real academic potential. You will see in later chapters that there may be ways to justify a shortcoming in one's grades. In chapter 6, we will discuss strategies for improving your GPA, even if you are graduating at the end of the current semester.

Another way that the term "Honors" is used is in reference to a special "Honors program" that students in some undergraduate

---

Some students quit graduate studies during or soon after their first year because they had entered graduate school with misconceptions about what would be expected of them, and they were not able to adjust to a new style of learning and evaluation. They believed that they were preparing well for graduate school by developing an ability to retain vast amounts of information from lectures or textbooks and to later recall it verbatim during tests. This style of studying gets them nowhere in graduate school.

programs are allowed to enrol in if they have an outstanding GPA. These students have Honors GPAs, and by virtue of this, they qualify to take special courses or seminars. Some undergraduate Honors programs require students to complete a special thesis. A student could have an Honors GPA, but for one reason or another choose not to enrol in an Honors program. As we have already discussed, it is not absolutely necessary to be in an Honors program in order to later get into graduate school, but it can help in many cases. When it is helpful, it can be for reasons different than you might think.

One might suspect that the impressive thing about students who are in Honors programs is their grades. After all, you have to have good grades to get into the Honors program in most departments, right? That is true. But it is often the case that once a student is in an Honors program it becomes easier to maintain good grades, because in some of these programs grades below B or B-plus are seldom given to out in the few special courses that only Honors students take. Even in other courses that non-Honors students also take, some professors hesitate to give anything less than a B or B-plus to an Honors student because they do not want anyone (such as the Honors Program Director or the student) to think that they are undermining the student's career plans.

Whether or not the perception that "easy grades" are administered to students in some Honors programs is truly accurate, many people believe that it is, and they may actually view a non-Honors student's GPA as more impressive than an equivalent GPA obtained by an Honors student! When I look at the transcripts of graduate school applicants, I ignore any Honors seminars or other courses that only Honors students are allowed to take, and I consider only the courses that non-Honors students also take. Some of my colleagues have told me that they do the same sort of thing. The point is that some admissions committee members may not care whether an applicant received a B or an A-plus in a special Honors seminar.

The real advantage of being in an Honors program stems from the purported aim of most of these programs: Honors programs are supposed to prepare aspiring students for some of the things that will be required of them in graduate school. For example, many Honors programs require students to do an independent research project and write a thesis. The Honors thesis can resemble a master's thesis in many respects, without the same standards of evaluation.

Doing independent research for an Honors thesis is an excellent way for some students to get their first glimpse of an important aspect of graduate school.

Although being in an Honors program is a good way to get useful experience and acquire a few skills relevant to graduate school, you can also attain these without being in an Honors program. The main difference is that if you are in an Honors program, you will probably be led by the hand and placed into beneficial situations. It is impressive when students without this advantage take matters into their own hands and seek other opportunities to obtain relevant experience. By doing so, they demonstrate some of the most important traits of a successful graduate student — good judgment and awareness, self-motivation, initiative, and creativity.

Of course, many Honors students possess these important traits, too, and I am not suggesting here that you should avoid being in an Honors program if you are qualified. Nor am I advising you against working harder to accomplish grades that will qualify you for enrolment in an Honors program. The point is simply that it is by no means *necessary* to be in an undergraduate Honors program in order to get into graduate school. Students who are not in an Honors program can volunteer to help professors with their research for a couple of semesters, or they can apply for part-time research-assistant jobs. In most fields, students can often get work or volunteer experience related to their intended areas of graduate study. If you are not qualified to be an Honors student because your grades don't measure up, do not worry. You are still in the game.

Summary   Two common misconceptions are that one must have outstanding grades to get into graduate school, and that outstanding grades are all one needs. Grades definitely *are* important, but so are many other factors. Students with only average or slightly above-average grades can get into graduate school if they have other strengths, and if they take certain steps and avoid mistakes during the application process.

There is considerable variability across graduate programs in terms of the importance of grades. Minimum entry requirements published in application packages and directories are usually not written in stone; exceptions may be made for students with other strengths.

Students with excellent grades, and those who are in Honors programs, should not assume that this is all they need to get into graduate school. These things can definitely help, but are neither necessary nor sufficient. Many students with excellent grades fail to get in because they come up short on other important dimensions, or because they make mistakes during the application process.

The following chapters will explain important aspects of graduate or professional school application and offer advice that students with or without excellent grades can use to improve their chances of getting in.

In recent years, most law, medical, and dental schools have subscribed to the services of central processing agencies. These agencies receive data and other materials from applicants and then summarize them into uniform formats before passing them on to the appropriate schools. These services ease both the burden on applicants and the clerical costs for the schools involved. Students should ascertain whether the programs they wish to apply to are among those that employ the services of these agencies. If so, they should write to the relevant agency to request Application Request Cards:

Law School Admission Service (LSAS)

Law Services, Box 2400

Newton, Pa., 18940-0977

American Medical College Application Service (AMCAS)

Section for Student Services

AAMC, 2450 N St. NW

Washington, D.C. 20037-1131

American Association of Dental Schools Application Service (AADSAS)

1625 Massachusetts Ave., NW, #101

Washington, D.C. 20036

Some of the schools that use these services charge their own application fees in addition to those charged by the central processing agencies.

Chapter 3

What You Need to Know
Before You Apply

Finding Out What Graduate or Professional School Is All About

Before you decide to apply to graduate school, or not to, you owe it to yourself to find out what graduate studies and an eventual career in your field of interest would be like. Many students apply to graduate school without really understanding how it differs from undergraduate school. Many successful applicants enter graduate school expecting that they will simply be taking more difficult courses. What they soon discover is that this is one of the *least* significant differences between undergraduate school and graduate school. Your first step, therefore, is to learn about the nature of graduate study in your field.

Some of the differences that exist between programs in various fields are obvious. For example, in most professional degree programs the graduate students admitted in any given year will generally work through a program in lock-step with each other, and individual faculty members do little or no direct supervision of individual students. By contrast, graduate work at the doctoral level in most nonprofessional fields is conducted under the supervision of an individual faculty member. The same is true for master's programs in some fields, but not in others.

One of the main differences between undergraduate and graduate school is the nature of the relationships you will have with professors and other students. The social environments are completely different. You may be working closely with professors who will treat you like a junior colleague, and expect you to behave like one. You may get to know some of the professors more as friends than as teachers, and you will probably call them by their first names.

There may be very few other students in the same graduate program as you, compared to the hundreds or thousands of others that were in the same undergraduate program. Some of you might be together on an almost daily basis for a few years, and you may find yourself having to work on major projects for extended periods with one or more other students. Even the ways in which you deal with secretaries and administrators will be different than when you were an undergraduate.

You will be part of a community and your success within it will depend to some extent on how well you are accepted by others and how well you feel you fit in. You will be highly visible most of the time. Those around you will get to know you very well. They will develop opinions about your personality and character based on the cumulation of all the interactions they have with you.

In sum, the social environment of graduate school favors participants who are reasonable, likeable, and who communicate well. Admissions committees and other graduate program faculty members want to fill their programs with students who fit this bill. These are among the most important dimensions on which candidates are evaluated. It is not enough to be smart. Unfortunately, this fact is largely unappreciated by the majority of applicants, who pay little or no attention to how they come across as a *person* to those who will be making decisions about their application.

Like it or not, your interpersonal skills will be on display at several different points in the application process. The fate of your application will depend largely on how these skills are perceived. This point will be repeated several times throughout the remainder of this book.

Ask your professors   The easiest way to begin learning the truth about graduate school in your field is to make an appointment with one of your professors and ask questions. There are many general things that just about any professor will be able to tell you about graduate school. Some professors will sincerely try to answer your questions (either because they are individuals who genuinely like helping others, or because you have flattered them by seeking their advice).

For reasons that remain a mystery to me, most students seem reluctant to visit with their professors outside of class, and when they do, it's almost always to deal with coursework. Most professors can be a good source of educational and career counselling and many enjoy speaking with students about such things. A conversation about graduate school with a professor can be illuminating for many students, who will discover things about graduate school that they had never heard of or imagined. This should not be surprising. After all, your professors have all gone to graduate school, and they may be currently involved in their own department's graduate programs.

Perhaps you cringe at the idea of approaching one of your professors because you have already had an uncomfortable experience with one who is especially grouchy, aloof, or arrogant. Rest assured, there are others you can seek counsel from who will not behave that way. There are specific faculty members in most departments who have the responsibility of serving as undergraduate advisors, and they are the first people whom you should seek to talk with about graduate studies. But don't stop there if none of these individuals seem approachable. You may be better off seeking advice from a professor you know a little better and whom you like.

Ask lots of questions and do not worry about appearing naive. Most professors realize that there is an information gap that prevents many undergraduates from finding out what's really involved in graduate school. Eventually, you will want to know about financial support, about the courses that you will have to take and the options that you will have in choosing courses, research requirements, comprehensive or area examinations, and the process of preparing and defending a thesis for an advanced degree.

Do not start panicking as you read this if you don't understand what all of these things are about. That is the whole reason for asking questions — to get the answers that will enable you to understand what is involved.

Some of the answers will reflect the kinds of written-in-stone policies that are nearly universally part of all programs in a particular field, whereas some others will merely reflect common practices that one would find in most programs. Still others may reflect how an individual professor tends to deal with his or her own graduate students. Ask about which things are fairly standard across graduate programs in your field and which are less common. It is at this point that most students first begin to understand that not all graduate programs in their discipline are alike.

Seek out and make use of career counsellors at your college or university. This might seem like an obvious way to find help, but for some mysterious reason, the existence and whereabouts of these important resource people are often unknown to students. Find out where to go on your campus for this type of advice and guidance. These people often know a lot about the ins-and-outs of graduate or professional school application. They might even be able to provide you with some of the books and other sources of information listed in the *Resources* section of this book.

A word of caution: **Never rely solely on the advice of just one individual!** Opinions vary a great deal among individual professors, even those within the same department who do similar research or teaching. That is simply that nature of academia. More so than in any other sector of society, academics and scholars are allowed to, in fact we are *expected* to, think differently.

Your professors are not all the same, and none of them is perfect. Some of them might not have well-informed opinions about graduate school and what it takes to apply successfully to a graduate program. Even among those who do know what they are talking about, professors often differ in their opinions about what is important for success in graduate school, or in a particular career afterwards. Even when two or more professors agree on a list of attributes that a good graduate student should possess, they may differ in how much emphasis each of them puts on particular attributes. It is important, therefore, that you seek advice and insight from several people.

Consider the source of any advice you receive. Are you talking to people who have been around for long enough to know how things work, both in their own department and in departments at different schools? Are they people who are likely to have offered similar advice in the past, and witnessed the outcome? Are they people who are actually involved in graduate training and research? If you are hearing the same sort of thing over and over again from credible sources, chances are it is good advice.

The book, *How to Get a Ph.D.*, by E.M. Phillips and D.S. Pugh does an excellent job of providing a realistic and practical understanding of the nature of postgraduate research for a doctorate degree (see the *Resources* section — General Advisement Guides — for complete reference information). The book is based primarily on the British system of postgraduate study, but much of it applies equally well to graduate schools in the United States, Canada, and elsewhere. I highly recommend this short and easy-to-read book to all students who are considering applying to a Ph.D. program.

Ask the "real experts"   Another excellent way to find out about graduate studies in your field is to talk with graduate students. (Of course, this might not be possible if your school does not offer a graduate program in your field). In many respects, current graduate students are the real experts. Do not assume that the kinds of things you see a graduate student doing in the capacity of teaching assistant for one of your professor's courses indicates how they spend most of their time, or what major responsibilities or concerns they have.

Chances are that you can find a graduate student who is willing to set you straight on several points about graduate school — things that you might not already be aware of. Most graduate students love giving advice and guidance to undergraduates. Sometimes this is because they are truly altruistic, and sometimes it is because they have budding academic egos that are nurtured by the opportunity to pass on their own "wisdom." Their first-hand accounts can turn out to be extremely helpful and important to you. Because they are involved in graduate studies *right now*, they are more acutely aware of what it is currently like to be a graduate student than are the professors who finished graduate school many years ago.

Ask these graduate students what a typical day is like for them. How much time do they spend in classes, or reading or writing, or conducting research? Ask them about other aspects of the graduate-student lifestyle. What do they like about it? What do they dislike? Why are they doing it? Talk to more than one or two students if you can, because each of them will have experiences that are somewhat different in certain respects. The commonalities among their accounts probably reflect things that would pertain to almost any graduate student in the same program, or in similar programs at other schools.

Is graduate school right for you?   Once you have a reasonable understanding of what graduate school is like you can make a well-informed decision about whether you should pursue it. You need to consider more than just your academic suitability, that is, how capable you are of studying hard and mastering new information and skills. You also have to consider whether your personality is right for graduate school.

Are you self-motivated and ambitious? As a graduate student, you will assume a greater responsibility for directing your education and training than you did as an undergraduate. You will not simply be fed information you must learn. You will have to seek much of the relevant knowledge on your own. You will teach, train, and supervise yourself in graduate school. The faculty, including your graduate supervisor if you have one, are there mostly to keep you on track, to facilitate your self-education, and serve as resources for you to take advantage of for knowledge and advice.

Depending on your field, you might have to do a tremendous amount of reading from scholarly books and journals. The faculty will not be evaluating your acquisition of new knowledge on a frequent or regular basis. That is your responsibility. No one will be checking to make sure you are doing this, so you will need to have self-discipline.

Do you have enough self-confidence? You will be expected to speak out in graduate classes to express your ideas and to challenge those of others. You won't be able to avoid public speaking in graduate school. You will occasionally have to occupy center stage for awhile, both in seminars and in more formal situations, such as when presenting your work to an audience of other students and faculty members. If you have a teaching assistantship, your duties might include giving undergraduate lectures or directing laboratories. You may have to present oral proposals for your thesis or dissertation work before you start it, and also present and defend the final work in a public forum after you are done.

Understanding How the Selection Process Works

One of the biggest impediments that many applicants to graduate school face is that they don't really understand how the application and selection processes work. They have no idea what is really going on with their application after they submit it. Without knowing how the selection process works, it is easy to make mistakes without realizing that you are doing so.

There are several criteria in addition to grades that contribute to the success or failure of a graduate or professional school application. In order to take advantage of these criteria and make up for a shortcoming in grades, it is important to know what goes into your application and to understand how the selection process generally works. Once you do, then some of the things that you can do to improve your own chances of success will be obvious. Knowledge is power, and ignorance can be fatal. Even if you have excellent grades, you are likely to fail in your attempt to get into graduate school if you look bad on the other dimensions on which applicants are evaluated.

As a word of caution, it is important that you understand at the outset that this section deals with commonalities that can be found among graduate programs in many fields. Despite these commonalities, every program is in some way unique and will differ from others

Students understandably focus on what their professors tell them, and they cannot reasonably be expected to anticipate the many important factors that are never explained to them. Even students who are confident that they understand how their application will be evaluated are usually wrong. Most faculty members who have served on graduate admissions committees would agree that a minority of applicants really know what is important and what is not. In fact, most students who are accepted into a program probably don't know the real reasons why they were successful!

in terms of the admissions requirements and methods of evaluating applicants. Accordingly, it warrants repeating here that you should be prepared to look beyond the general information and advice given in this book in order to deal with specific details when you are applying to particular programs in a particular field.

Be careful not to overestimate the accuracy of your current understanding of the selection process. And beware that many misconceptions that students have are inadvertently perpetuated by professors. It's not that the advice professors give is bad — it is rather that many important things are not fully explained. For example, students are seldom told that how they come across as a *person* is crucial.

Who ultimately makes the selections?   Most universities have a Faculty or a School of Graduate Studies that plays a role in the administration of certain aspects of all departmental graduate programs at that institution. Often the Faculty or School plays only a minor role in the selection process beyond establishing minimum grade requirements or some other standards that apply to all of the graduate programs. Most of the selection work will be done by faculty members in the specific department to which you are applying.

Most programs have an admissions committee (often also referred to as a *selection committee*) consisting of a few faculty members who meet each year after the application deadline to pore over the pile of applications. Most programs also have a Graduate Program Director, who is also on the admissions committee. Most departments appoint their own admissions committee, and the composition of the group, as well as policies and procedures for making selections, will vary from one program to another.

The general aim of most admissions committees is to provide a rating of each of the current applicants and to ultimately make the decision of who is acceptable for the program. This process usually involves ranking the applicants on the basis of their overall application package, and eliminating some of the lower ranking applicants from the competition.

Once your application file is complete, it might sit amongst a pile of other files for several days, or even weeks, before anyone looks at it. In some programs, especially those in which students do not, strictly speaking, study and train under the supervision of a single faculty member, the admissions committee makes the final decision of whether to accept or reject an applicant.

In most doctoral programs, and in master's programs that have a research thesis, students do their work under the supervision of a sponsoring faculty member (a graduate supervisor). In many of these programs, the admissions committee plays a relatively minor role in deciding whether individual applicants will be accepted or rejected.

There is considerable variance among programs in terms of just how much of the final decision-making is done by the admissions committee. One might assume from the name given to the admissions committee that their primary task is to decide who will be admitted to the program. In fact, they are usually responsible for administering departmental or university policy and implementing procedures for dealing with the entire admissions process, which involves much more than just selecting applicants.

After the files are collected by a graduate program secretary (this is usually the person to whom you are asked to submit application materials), they may be studied briefly by the admissions committee, and then the acceptable ones are distributed to the faculty members who the applicants have indicated they would like to have as their graduate supervisor. These individual faculty members are the ones who ultimately decide who gets in and who doesn't.

After the faculty members have gone through the files of the applicants who have indicated specific interest in having them for a supervisor, they might return the files to the admissions committee along with a list of applicants they would like to accept. An individual professor might have five or ten or even two dozen students applying each year to do graduate studies under his or her supervision, and from among that group of applicants he or she might choose one or two ... or perhaps none! Obviously, in order to be a successful applicant, you must do some things that will place you above your competition in the eyes of the prospective supervisor.

Many faculty members will still accept applicants despite a poor rating from the admissions committee. This is usually because they are impressed by some aspect of the applicant that is more important to them than to the admissions committee. Perhaps through direct correspondence with the applicant they have come to suspect that the grades or standardized-test scores do not reflect this student's true ability or potential. They use their own criteria for deciding whether to sponsor individual applicants. The next subsection deals with some of those criteria and how you can take advantage of them to increase your chances of being accepted into a graduate program (also see chapters 7 and 8).

It is important that you understand what we have just discussed — that in many programs, a faculty member's consent or desire to serve as an applicant's graduate supervisor is the main determinant of acceptance into the program. As we will see, there is a great deal at stake for professors who decide to supervise your graduate studies, so you must keep in mind that they will decide to take you on as their student only if they think it is in their best interest to do so. They will be comparing you to other applicants who also wish to do graduate work with them.

Students need to understand what is at stake for the prospective supervisor. You have probably heard the phrase "Publish or perish." In many disciplines, the status of a faculty member depends to a great extent on how prolific they are in presenting or publishing their work. The output of many professors depends primarily upon the quality of the team they have working with them, and that team may consist mostly of graduate students. Choosing the right graduate student can be a tremendous benefit to a faculty member's career. Selecting a bad graduate student can result in a significant impediment to progress in one's research program, which can in turn slow career advancement.

Individual professors often put less emphasis on undergraduate grades when selecting new graduate students than do admissions committees. This means that you have several other ways of making yourself the winning applicant. You must learn to recognize and seize these opportunities.

It is so important that you remember this that I must repeat it again: In many graduate programs, it is the the prospective supervisor who has the most influence on whether or not you get in. Therefore, much of your efforts should aim to convince this person that you would be successful in graduate studies and that he or she would benefit from having you as a graduate student. For the remainder of this book, that individual faculty member who would serve as your mentor and supervisor during your graduate studies will be referred to as the *"prospective supervisor."*

Understand what "they" are looking for "They" refers to either the members of the admissions committee or the prospective graduate supervisors. As eluded to previously, the members of the admissions committee are looking to bring the most promising people into their graduate programs. Similarly, the prospective supervisor is looking to bring the most promising people into his or her own individual research program.

The key here is the emphasis on *people*. This can be a difficult notion for students to appreciate, for it is widely assumed that the competition for entry into graduate school is ultimately fair, and therefore, that it must be based solely on objective criteria, such as grades. Of course, grades are important, but there is a great deal at stake both for the program as a whole and for the faculty members who supervise graduate students. It is important to them that they admit people who possess certain other nonobjective credentials and positive personality traits.

Contrary to popular belief, most graduate admissions committees select applicants to their programs according to the credo: "Grades don't tell the whole story! "

One of the first questions that almost any admissions committee will ask is whether the applicant's goals and interests match the objectives and specialities of the program. It is easy to spot the applicants who didn't do any advance research about the programs to which they are applying. Many students underestimate how specialized some graduate programs are. The reason for this specialization is because a graduate program can provide the best training only in areas in which its own faculty members are experts. For example, one graduate program in Agriculture might be particularly strong in animal nutrition, whereas another one might specialize in plant physiology, and yet another in animal breeding and genetics. Most would have more than one area of strength.

After determining that the applicant's intentions match those of the program, the admissions committee considers other things. As usual, there will be differences among various programs and across disciplines in terms of the most important factors. Doctoral programs may be looking for evidence that the applicant has already demonstrated an ability to perform beyond the undergraduate level by earning a masters degree.

Students in some sciences, such as Biology or Chemistry and many others, have plenty of opportunities to participate in original research while they are still undergraduates. This research experience is something that master's programs in those fields are looking for in applicants. In these fields graduate work at the master's level focuses on the research thesis. But the same is not true in other fields. In Mathematics or Physics, for example, it takes a few years of coursework at the graduate level before students can be expected to understand the concepts necessary to participate in original research. Master's programs in Mathematics and Physics, therefore, place more emphasis on a student's academic record and standardized-test scores.

Almost any graduate program will give some consideration to evidence pertaining to the applicant's character or personality. The members of the admissions committee have a vested interest in ensuring that they only allow mature, polite, and generally agreeable people into their program. They may spend hundreds of hours in relative proximity to graduate students, so it is only reasonable that they would avoid people who are unpleasant or annoying. Character and personality will be even more important to prospective supervisors, because they know that they will have a great deal of interaction with any new graduate student over the next few years.

Many students fail to understand something that should really be quite obvious: Someone will agree to supervise your graduate studies only if there is something in it for them. Graduate supervisors are people, too. Supervisors may be looking for evidence that you possess special qualities or skills that will help them with their own research. This is the give-and-take nature of the graduate student/supervisor relationship. Everyone has specific needs, and that includes faculty members who supervise graduate students and allow them to participate in ongoing research or other scholarly work.

The graduate school applicant must determine the needs of the prospective supervisor and address them at every step of the way through the application process. This theme will be repeated throughout this book.

Summary   In most doctoral programs, and in master's programs that have a research thesis, graduate students do their work under the supervision of a particular faculty member. In many of these programs, the admissions committee does not decide who will ultimately be accepted into the program — rather, they decide who is *acceptable*. It is then up to individual professors to decide whether to accept particular applicants.

Many professors will accept certain applicants despite a poor rating from the admissions committee, so long as they believe that they will benefit from having these students. Most graduate school applicants will have to impress both the admissions committee and the prospective supervisor in order to get in. Therefore, applicants must determine the specific needs of the prospective supervisor, and the general needs of the program as a whole, and then address these needs at every step of the way through the application process.

Basic Components of a Graduate or Professional School Application

Most graduate programs require applicants to submit most or all of the following items by a certain deadline: 1) application forms, 2) official transcripts of university or college grades, 3) official scores on one or more standardized test, 4) two or more letters of recommendation (three letters is most common), and 5) a personal statement, or an essay (or essays) in response to a specific question (or questions), usually pertaining to the applicant's educational or career goals.

A few programs in special fields require additional items, such as a curriculum vitae (discussed in chapter 9), or a portfolio or dossier, but the five that are listed above and described briefly below are the most common. In chapters 6 and 7, we will deal with each of them in much greater detail so that you will know how to produce a winning application package.

Application forms   You can expect to have to fill out either one or two application forms for each program. For programs requiring two forms, one of them is usually a university-wide application form — one that is filled out by applicants to any graduate program at that university. The other application form is for the specific department or program to which they are applying.

Much of the information will be the same on the two forms. Still, you must be sure that you fill out *all* of the line items on *both* forms. They will be going into different files in different offices, so both of them must be complete. In addition to providing standard biographical data, you will be asked to indicate the program of study to which you are applying, and to provide details about your academic history. You may also be asked about your employment history and relevant professional and research experience. Most applications also ask for the name, title, and address of three or more referees. There also may be instructions and space provided for your personal statement on the application form.

There is more to properly filling out application forms than simply providing the right information. Many students make mistakes while filling out application forms without realizing they are doing anything wrong. More on this later.

Transcripts of undergraduate grades   The undergraduate GPA is almost universally, but not quite so, a heavily weighted factor in the decisions of admissions committees. Admissions committees often weigh a student's grades for the final two years of undergraduate school somewhat more heavily than the grades from their first two years. There is also some attention paid to the particular courses that the applicants have taken and to their performance in a few select courses. For example, it is important that students of Psychology take one or more courses in experimental design and statistics for behavioral research, and that they do reasonably well in those courses.

The main concern at this initial stage of evaluation is whether the applicant meets the minimum grade requirements for entry into the program. Unless there is something else that is special about the applicant whose GPA is below the minimum criterion, that person is usually eliminated from the competition. There are usually few applicants who fail to meet minimum grade requirements, so the admissions committee is likely to *rank* the applicants according to their grades, paying particular attention to those with exceptionally high grades, or those with grades that are very low relative to the rest of the applicants.

Most applicants think that the issue of grades is where the competition to get into graduate school ends, but as you will see in a moment, it's really only where it begins! If you are a student with mediocre grades, then take heart, because one aim of this book is to show you how to be a "special" applicant who will not be screened out at this point merely because of a less-than-exceptional GPA.

Minimum grade requirements range from quite high in some programs to surprisingly low in others. Higher minimum entry requirements are characteristic of programs that receive a large number of applications each year and can accept only a small fraction. But the higher requirements shouldn't be assumed to reflect higher quality graduate education. Just because a lot of students apply to these programs, this doesn't necessarily mean that they provide better training.

Scores on standardized tests (GRE, LSAT, GMAT, etc.) Most graduate and professional degree programs (but not all of them) require applicants to submit official scores on one or more standardized tests. These tests provide an objective basis for comparing students' academic aptitude. They are designed to assess academic knowledge and skills relevant to graduate studies. The scores are thought to be one measure of academic aptitude that is not influenced by the huge variation that exists in the grading standards and procedures of different courses, professors, departments, faculties, and schools. The rationale is that everyone writes an equivalent test and all tests are graded the same way. Thus, the playing field is level for all participants.

Letters of recommendation   Unlike GPA and standardized test scores, which are objective measures of a student's aptitude, letters of recommendation provide nonobjective assessments of the student. Most programs require two or three letters of recommendation from people who can attest to the fact that you possess qualities that will enable you to excel in graduate school. The most effective letters are from professors who are familiar with you and your scholarly or research capabilities, or from professionals or other qualified individuals from outside your college or university who have a good basis for being able to provide such an assessment.

Few students anticipate far enough in advance that they will need two or three strong letters of recommendation, and most end up scrambling at the end to find someone, perhaps *anyone*, who will write one for them. It takes time and planning to ensure that you receive effective endorsements. Without knowing what makes a letter of recommendation effective or ineffective, many students end up asking the wrong people for them. In chapter 7, we will discuss various ways of arranging for the most effective letters of recommendation.

The personal statement (or essay)   Another nonobjective criterion for assessing an applicant's potential is the personal statement (also sometimes called the *statement of purpose, letter of intent,* or *biographical essay*). One purpose of this statement is to explain why you want to enrol in a particular graduate program. Another of its purposes is to describe your qualifications. As you will see later in chapter 7, admissions committees are not so much interested in your specific reasons or qualifications as much as they want to ascertain from your statement whether you have realistic goals with respect to what the program will do for you and what a career in this field would be like.

Not all graduate programs require a personal statement. Some programs, particularly professional degree programs, ask applicants to write a few short essays in response to specific questions. Other programs instead have sections on the application form that ask for the same information that one would normally provide in a personal statement.

Admissions committees look closely for evidence in the personal statement that the applicant possesses important positive attributes that will be needed for success in their programs, and in a career afterwards. Importantly, they are also looking for evidence of negative attributes, and when such concerns are raised by the content or style of the applicant's personal statement, it can lead to rejection.

Although the personal statement will in some cases mean the difference between an applicant being accepted or rejected, many students fail to take this part of their application seriously enough. The most common mistake is to hastily write the statement without enough preparation. Some students spend only a few hours preparing their statements instead of the weeks necessary for most people to do a proper job of it. And in those few hours they can ruin their entire application.

> *In addition to the five basic components that most programs require, there are also a number of "hidden" criteria. Although not specified, they are nonetheless given a great deal of consideration. One of the aims of this book is to reveal some of these hidden criteria and suggest ways to help you satisfy them.*

Summary Each of the five basic components of graduate or professional school applications is dealt with in detail in later chapters. For now, it is important that you understand some basic points about them:

The quality of a student's transcripts is determined by more than just the grade-point-average. In most disciplines, there are certain courses that are more important than others, and the grades obtained in the last few semesters may be weighed more heavily than those obtained in the first year or two of an undergraduate program.

Many students make mistakes filling out application forms without realizing they are doing anything wrong. There is more to properly filling out forms than simply providing the right information.

Some individuals will look closely at your scores on standardized tests. They will try determine whether these scores concur with, or contradict, what your grades suggest about your academic abilities.

Most programs require three letters of recommendation. Students need to understand what factors make a letter of recommendation effective or ineffective, so that they can take steps in advance to ensure that they end up with good letters. Planning for letters of recommendation should ideally begin months, or even years, before the letters will actually be needed.

Most students seriously underestimate the importance of their personal statements or essays. As a result, they fail to give sufficient time and attention to this part of their application. An effective personal statement will take most students a few weeks to prepare, but a majority of them will only spend a few hours.

Financing Graduate Study

It is normal to feel twinges of excitement while preparing for your graduate school applications. But the topic of financing is bound to come up eventually, and when it does, the excitement may diminish somewhat. There can be considerable expense associated with years of graduate school. The good news is that, in many respects, it is easier to finance graduate school than undergraduate school, and you will soon learn that your situation probably is not as bleak as you first assumed.

Begin your financial plan by estimating both the annual costs of (probably full-time) graduate study, and all sources of financial support that you are certain to have. Your total costs include tuition and other school fees and expenses, as well as all other living expenses (rent, groceries, clothes, etc.). If you have been avoiding certain expenses by living in your parents' home, this may soon end because there is a good chance that you will end up going to graduate school in a different city.

When you calculate your anticipated sources of financial support, you probably should *not* include any expected earnings from employment, either full-time or part-time. In most graduate and professional programs, student are expected to pursue full-time studies and are generally advised not to work at a part-time job, unless it is one that takes up very little time, or has some pedagogical function related to the program of study. Many programs do not permit part-time enrolment.

It should be noted, however, that in some programs it is not unusual for graduate students to pursue *part-time study* while they continue to work full-time at a regular job. This is more common in programs that cater to students who have been working in a career for some time since obtaining a college degree, and are seeking to upgrade their knowledge and credentials.

For most students, the estimated annual costs of graduate school drastically exceeds the total amount of *certain* financial support. Luckily, compared to undergraduate school, graduate school is easier to finance for most students. This is because there is simply a greater variety of ways to get your hands on the money you need for graduate school than there was for undergraduate school. Numerous guides, directories, and handbooks are listed in the *Resources* section (Funding Guides) to help you explore your options.

Sources of financial support   The purpose of this section is to familiarize you with some of the more common types of financial aid. Nearly all graduate students receive financial aid from at least one of the following sources, but the percentage from each category varies widely across disciplines.

Research assistantships, teaching assistantships, traineeships.   Many graduate students make a decent income working as research assistants or teaching assistants. Because most of them manage to get assistantships doing work related to their field of study, there are the added benefits of gaining some useful experience and something to add to their résumé.

The workload can vary a great deal. I earned about $13,500 one year working as a teaching assistant for two semesters and a research assistant for the summer. All I did as a teaching assistant was mark exams and tutor students for a couple of hours each week. As a research assistant, I just worked on my thesis research. Clearly, I had it pretty easy! In most other departments the students are paid much less and do a great deal more work as teaching assistants or research assistants. Even in those cases, when their salary is considered in light of the hours spent working on teaching assistant or research assistant duties, they are making more money in less time than they could at most part-time off-campus jobs.

Scholarships, fellowships, grants, bursaries.   An amazing number of graduate scholarships and fellowships are awarded each year by various governments, private groups, and by the graduate schools themselves. The competition for most scholarships and fellowships is based mostly on the quality of the students' grades. In some respects this is unfortunate, because as we have already discussed, undergraduate grades are not always the best predictor of performance in graduate school. Ideally, the scholarship money should be going to students who are most likely to make it a good investment by excelling in graduate school. The problem is that some graduate programs place very little emphasis on coursework and in-class testing, and this is why undergraduate grades can sometimes lack predictive power.

But some awarding committees do make a concerted effort to consider factors other than grades, and therefore, most students who do not already have a scholarship should consider applying for every award for which they are qualified to compete. The process of awarding scholarships and fellowships can be extremely capricious at times — just like the process of selecting applicants to a graduate program! Keep this in mind if you ever fail in a bid to win a scholarship or to get into a graduate program. You should not take the results of these applications to be a reliable measure of your ability or potential (unless of course, the result is success, in which case you should believe that you deserve it).

At most universities, students apply for internal sources of financial aid at the time of application to the graduate program. In many cases, there is nothing to submit beyond what is already in your application package, although there are occasional exceptions. At some schools there is a separate, and usually earlier, financial aid application deadline. Find out as early as possible about the procedures for applying for internal sources of funding at the schools that interest you. Some financial aid forms request special information that is not part of the graduate school application, and in some cases, they may require a special essay or personal statement.

Private and government scholarship competitions have application deadlines at various times throughout the year. For some of them, the competition is only open to students who are already enrolled in graduate school. For others, you can apply before you are officially accepted into a program. Of course, no award will be conferred if you fail to get into graduate school. On the other hand, your chances of being accepted into almost any graduate program will increase considerably if you have been awarded a graduate scholarship or fellowship from a government or private source, as long as it is an award that you can hold at the university in question.

Many scholarships exist specifically for students studying in a certain field, or for certain student populations, such as ethnic minority groups (see the *Resources* section — Funding Guides). Moreover, many awards have citizenship restrictions, and some must be held at a school within the student's home state or province. This is important information to have before applying for any scholarship, because there is a good chance that you will be choosing between graduate programs located in regions far from each other.

Tuition and other fee waivers. Some graduate schools are more generous than others with these forms of financial aid. Even when it is available, the financial assistance is not as substantial as a stipend to cover the basic costs of living, but in combination with one or more of the other forms of financial aid, it can help a great deal. International students sometimes receive special consideration for tuition and other fee waivers. An international student fee remission usually means that the student is charged academic fees at the same rate as a student with domestic citizenship. If you think that you might qualify, inquire early enough to make sure that you don't miss an early deadline.

Loans. Many students begin their financial planning for graduate school by assuming that loans will constitute the main part of their support. It might turn out this way for some graduate students, but sometimes the main reason why is because this is precisely the way that they planned it! It can be a kind of self-fulfilling prophecy. Unfortunately, students sometimes fail to become aware of all the potential sources of financial aid for which they can compete. I think that everyone should do what they can to obtain financial support in another way before they resign themselves to having to borrow for graduate school.

Loan support does offer at least one advantage over some of the alternatives, such as teaching assistantships or research assistantships. It gives you more control over how you spend your time. You will be busy with your own work when you are a graduate student, and you may appreciate that you have borrowed for your education if it means you don't have to wash test tubes as a research assistant.

Many graduate students will find it much easier to get loans and other forms of aid than it was when they were undergraduates. This is because many forms of aid are based on a student's financial *need*, which in turn is based on the difference between the cost of going to school and the financial contribution that is expected from the student's family. Most students are declared as *dependents* by their parents while they are undergraduates, and therefore, familial financial support is expected to come from the student's own assets and income, as well as those of the parents.

It is easier to qualify as an *independent* student while you are in graduate school, which means that financial support is expected from your personal assets and income alone (plus your spouse's if you happen to be married). Your assets and income are probably substantially less than those of your parents, so your calculated financial need will be greater as an independent graduate student. Just make sure that your parents are not claiming you as a dependent for tax purposes.

There are vast amounts of financial aid available, and you will probably qualify for some of it. In addition to the ample federal loan programs in both the U.S. and Canada, several states and provinces have loan programs that augment the available national funding. The interest rates are low, and for many subsidized loans there is no interest accrual during the loan period.

Summary   The key to financing graduate school is to start looking into the various possibilities as early as possible. Two problems seem to occur most often to prevent students from getting the financial support they need: A lack of understanding of the full range of funding sources, and insufficient or late planning. There are many ways to get your hands on the money you need to go to graduate school, but if you don't begin researching the options months or even years before you will be applying to graduate programs, you are likely to miss some of the best opportunities.

Students should begin to inquire about financial-aid competitions at least ten months before they expect to be applying to graduate school. Private and government scholarship competitions have application deadlines at various times throughout the year, and many of the scholarships and other awards that are administered by universities or departments have application deadlines before the graduate program application deadlines.

A professional master's degree prepares students for a career in a particular area, or else it enhances their skills in an existing career. Accordingly, the professional master's degree is generally a final degree. A master's degree in a research area may also be an endpoint in a student's graduate education, but often it is merely a stepping-stone on the way to a Ph.D.

Chapter 4

Making the Right Choices

The purpose behind graduate and professional degree programs is to turn promising students into competent specialists well-suited to a specific range of careers. Accordingly, the most important consideration when choosing which degree to pursue is whether it will give you the qualifications you need for the career you want. The title of the particular degree obtained, however, often obscures the specialized nature of the competence that is acquired in obtaining it. Individuals with the same degree in the same field may differ a great deal in terms of the nature of their acquired expertise.

The amount of success you have in applying to graduate or professional school will depend to a large extent on whether you pick the right programs. **The programs you apply to must match your specific objectives in terms of the kinds of training you want and the type of career you are hoping to have afterward.** Do not underestimate the importance of this match. It is one of the main things that admissions committees are looking for when they evaluate applicants to their programs.

In many fields, the importance of making choices based on one's specific interests and objectives goes beyond the selection of the right graduate program. Doctoral programs involve independent research, which is conducted under the supervision and guidance of an individual faculty member. Master's students in some programs also do a research thesis under the guidance of a graduate supervisor. **These programs are particularly concerned with matching students with faculty.** This matching is usually done of the basis of common research interests; no matter how impressive their qualifications are, applicants are sure to be rejected if they cannot be properly matched with a faculty member. This is not an issue in master's programs where students do not have a specific graduate supervisor.

There is an important distinction between *terminal* and *non-terminal* master's programs. A nonterminal master's degree usually precedes entry into a doctoral program (although there is an increasing number of doctoral programs that do not require a master's degree). By contrast, terminal programs specifically train people for occupations that require only a master's degree. Therefore, you need at least a general idea of your career objectives in order to choose between a terminal and nonterminal master's degree. You will probably choose a nonterminal master's program, unless you know for sure that you won't want to pursue a doctorate later on.

Making the right choices requires that you first have a good idea of the type of career you want. If you are uncertain about the career options available to someone with an advanced degree in your field, talk with a career counsellor. Your professors might also be good sources of information, especially on academic careers.

Choosing the Right Graduate Program

If you are considering seeking an advanced degree, you need to understand that programs that offer the same degree can be very different in terms of the types of training they offer and the types of specialists they are designed to create. For example, one program in

Economics might offer expertise in econometrics, microeconomics, macroeconomics, economic development and planning, or financial and monetary economics, whereas another program might have its strengths in the areas of labor economics, environmental and natural resources economics, public economics, or industrial organization. The particular strengths of a program will depend on the expertise of its faculty members. Programs vary in terms of how flexible they are in permitting the creation of thesis research outside of their particular realms of specialization.

The importance of choosing a program that matches your objectives means that before you can choose an appropriate graduate program you should decide what type of career you want to pursue afterwards. It is beyond the scope of this book to offer detailed advice on how to go about making that decision. Apart from going to your library and researching the kinds of careers available to someone with an advanced degree in your field, the best way to learn about career options is from faculty members of your department, as was recommended in chapter 3, or from career counsellors, if such resource people exist at your school.

Where to begin your search   The reference sections of most college libraries have calendars or brochures for graduate schools across North America and abroad. This is a good place to begin, but remember that these brochures are a form of advertising and will, therefore, paint a rosy picture of the program, the university, the campus, the city, etc.

Most college libraries will also have the most current volumes of *Peterson's Guides to Graduate and Professional Programs* (see the *Resources* section — Graduate Program Directories). These comprehensive directories list almost all of the professional and graduate programs in North America, along with their areas of expertise, and information on such things as the number of faculty members, and who to contact for an application or other information. There are separate volumes for Business, Health, Education, and Law; Engineering and Applied Sciences; Biological and Agricultural Sciences; Humanities, Arts, and Social Sciences; and for the Physical Sciences and Mathematics. See the *Resources* section for more ways to find information you need to create a list of potential programs.

If you have access to the Internet, you can find even more information this way. There are now thousands of graduate programs with sites on the World-Wide-Web. You can find links to all sorts of information about a program, its faculty and students, and about the university, the city, and much more. Some of them allow you to download their application package.

Some programs are more competitive than others, in terms of accepting only students with exceptional credentials, and this is another important factor to consider when choosing where to apply. Students with mediocre grades and standardized test scores may not have much chance of getting into one of the more competitive and high-profile programs.

It may not be prudent to spend time and money applying to programs are clearly not realistic for you in light of your qualifications, but there are likely to be dozens of other programs that also offer the education and training you seek and that are considerably less competitive. Do not assume that you will receive an inferior graduate education in a lower-profile, less competitive graduate program.

> *Some programs attract huge numbers of highly-qualified applicants each year, whereas others attract fewer students or students with somewhat weaker credentials. Why are some programs much more competitive than others? Contrary to what most people assume, the more competitive programs don't always provide better training than the less competitive programs. As with many other things that reflect supply and demand, the prestige of a program can be unrelated to the real value of what it has to offer.*

Use the brochures, calendars, directories, and web pages to compile a list of potential programs that offer the degree that interests you, but do not use them as your only sources of information in deciding where to apply. They do not have all of the information you need to make this decision.

After you have compiled a tentative list of potential programs to consider, seek advice from as many people you can. If there are one or two professors in your department whom you look up to, start by getting their advice. But do not stop there. If possible, get statistics on the number of degrees granted versus the number of students admitted. This ratio should be high — as close to 1:1 as possible.

Is it the right place for you?   It is important that you feel comfortable in a program. Try to get an idea of what the working and social environments are like so you can ask yourself whether you are likely to fit in.

For many students, the beginning of graduate studies marks the first time they have moved away from their home towns and the comfort of familiar surroundings, leaving behind family and friends. If you have already made this kind of move before, such as when you entered college, then you probably recall how the first few months felt as you struggled to adjust. It probably took you a while to feel like you fit in and to meet new friends. This was a stressful time, and to make the jump to graduate school you will likely have to go through the same kind of thing all over again, although it may be easier this time.

The more suited your new environment is to your personality, the more likely it is that your transition to graduate school will go smoothly. It is important, therefore, to get a first-hand look at where you will be doing your work for the next few years if you are accepted and choose to enrol.

The best way to get certain kinds of information about specific graduate programs is to visit them. You should make every effort possible to pay a visit to at least those programs that interest you the most. Find out who the Graduate Program Director is and contact that person a couple of weeks in advance. Let them know who you are, what days you expect to be visiting the campus, and ask to make an appointment with them or with someone else in order to find out more about their program.

Find out as much as you can about what it is like to be a graduate student there. Visit as many faculty members and students as you can. The graduate students will be the best source of information about what it is like to be in the program. You must be careful, however, not to put too much stock into the reports of only a single graduate student. Talk to several of them and look for points of general consensus. The danger in speaking with only one or two is that their attitudes and opinions may not be representative of the majority of students in that program. Some students fall into unhappy circumstances for no reasons other than those of their own doing, yet they blame their problems on others or on their environment.

When you meet the graduate students, do you like them? This is important because these students will be your compatriots for the next few years. You will need to feel comfortable in their company. You may come to depend on them for moral support and friendship. It is more difficult to succeed in graduate school if you are alone, without a good social support group.

Ask to see where you will be doing most of your work, and check out other resources such as the library, computing centers, etc. Find out what areas of town the graduate students tend to live in and visit those neighborhoods. Take some time to see the city and get a feel for what it would be like to live there for a few years. An added advantage of making this trip is that you will be much more prepared and adjust more quickly if you do end up going there for graduate school.

> *There is a lot more to choosing the right program than just finding one that offers the degree you need and the specialization you want.*

General impressions versus specific factors   You will collect a great deal of information about a graduate school when you visit, and sorting through all of it later on will seem like a daunting task. But it is well worth the effort. With so many things to consider, there are sure to be many positives as well as a few negatives. What information is most important and what is less critical?

Your advance research told you what kind of training and degrees the program offers, and presumably, these are among the main reasons why you have considered this program. Did you obtain any information that would either confirm or disconfirm that the program is still appropriate?

Unless there are only a few programs that offer graduate training in the field you seek, I recommend at this point that you begin to narrow down your search. Begin by focusing on the general impressions that you are left with. Pay less attention to the specifics for now; it is better to leave details for later consideration (hopefully, when you find yourself choosing between two or more programs that have accepted you!).

Of course, the general impression that you have of a program will reflect the combined influence of many specific details. So, what you should do is not so much ignore the specific details completely; rather, you just should not consider each of them in isolation. You should add them all together — applying appropriate weight to specific negatives and positives — and consider only the final sum, for now.

There may be one exception to the notion that one should mostly pay attention to the general impression that they are left with after visiting a graduate school. This exception has to do with the people who you meet there, especially the graduate students. No matter how perfect the match is between your educational and career goals and the strengths of the program, no matter how much you like the campus, the city, and the climate, you are likely to experience difficulties coping with the demands of graduate school if you are not able to tolerate your peers. Of course, the idea here is not that you need to like everyone you meet. But the group as a whole should be one you can identify with and easily feel a part of.

Trust your instincts when deciding whether a particular program is right for you. If you do not like what you see or the people you meet, if you hear a little voice telling you to stay away, then you should. Do not hesitate to remove that school from your list.

Do not apply to places where you don't want to go. A recent student of mine had very good grades and standardized test scores but was otherwise ill-prepared when the time came to apply for graduate school. The lack of preparation was reflected in the outcome: He was rejected by all the programs that appealed to him most. He was, however, offered admission at one program, and he enrolled there, even though it was the program he desired least. He spent the next four years studying and training in a field that wasn't really what he wanted. He would have been better off refusing the offer of admission and focusing on taking steps to prepare effectively for application to a more suitable place the next year.

What to do if you cannot visit   Many program brochures and web sites provide a description of the city, local cultures, and even climatological features of the region. Some brochures and calendars describe the department's general philosophy toward research and in-class testing. But you miss out on so much of the real feel of a place when you are unable to experience it first-hand. For one thing, the brochures, calendars, and web sites will not list any negative aspects of a program.

You can learn a lot about a program by calling people in that program and asking them a few questions, but you can't talk to enough different people this way. Perhaps someone at your current school knows something about some of the programs on your list. A particular program might have a reputation among people in the field (these reputations will tend to be more valid than most of those that exist among the general population). Are any of your professors familiar with any of the schools? Do they know any of the faculty there? One of your professors might have gone to graduate school there!

Just because you can't visit a program, this should not stop you from contacting some of the graduate students who are currently in that program. You could ask the Graduate Program Director to help get you in touch with a graduate student, preferably someone who has been around long enough and has the experience needed to provide well-informed answers to your questions.

Electronic mail is now available to almost every graduate student in North America and even to most undergraduate students. This is a convenient way of corresponding with graduate students in a prospective program. But some of the advantages of a real conversation over the phone are absent in email correspondence. Use email to ask your graduate-student contact a few questions, but at some point you should try to arrange a time to phone when they would be willing to talk with you. Many subtleties that would be present in a phone conversation are lost in electronic mail.

Do not plan to call more than once, unless you are invited to call again. You do not want to be a pest. Do not flood them with email either. Keep in mind that this student may discuss your correspondence with the graduate supervisor and thereby influence the decision concerning your application.

> *Don't listen to anyone who tells you that you will always receive better training at a high-profile school like Harvard or Johns Hopkins than you will at a university with a lower profile. This does not have to be the case. The general reputation of a school can often be totally irrelevant. Be aware that many well-educated people also share common misconceptions about the relation between a school's general reputation and the quality of its graduate or professional training.*

Summary   Graduate programs offer specialized training in only certain areas. In order to choose the right program, therefore, you should first have some idea of what type of specialized training you seek. Ask career counsellors and professors to help you consider the alternatives. Consult the *Resources* section for guidebooks to exploring career options.

Once you know what you are looking for, you must do comprehensive research into what various programs have to offer. There are numerous sources of information, many of which are listed in the *Resources* section of this book. The best approach is to use a combination of sources, including various program directories and the Internet.

Some programs are much more competitive than others. Before you invest time and money in applying to a particular program, give some consideration to whether you have a reasonable chance of success based on the competitiveness of the program and the strength of your credentials.

It is important to feel comfortable where you decide to go to graduate school. Information that will help you judge whether the social and work environments of a program are suited to your personality and style can only be acquired through a visit. Every effort should be made to visit at least those programs that interest you the most. Meet with several faculty members and graduate students to get different perspectives on various facets of the program. It is important, in general, that you like the people you meet.

If you cannot visit a program, you can still use the phone and electronic mail to correspond with individuals there. Also seek advice from professors and graduate students in your current department who may know something about the programs that interest you.

Choosing the Right Graduate Supervisor

Graduate study and research at the doctoral level are typically conducted under the supervision of a faculty member who is responsible for guiding the student through the program and training them in various skills and knowledge of the field. In some disciplines, students also study under a particular graduate supervisor at the master's level. There are other variations on this, too. For example, students in some master's programs complete a year of coursework before being assigned to a graduate supervisor. Another system used by some has new graduate students alternating on a rotational basis among different faculty during the first few semesters.

In some programs, students are more or less "assigned" to supervisors, whereas in others the match-making is mostly left up to the student and is largely done *before* enrolling in the program. As we discussed earlier, an important consideration of selection committees is whether an applicant can be matched with a willing faculty member. Whether it is up to you to find a graduate supervisor or you are assigned to one, you need to know who the potential supervisors are before you can decide where to apply.

The reason why some programs have new graduate students rotate between supervisors before settling with one is to give the students a broad exposure to different viewpoints, approaches or methods of inquiry, or facets of the discipline. It is *not* so that the students can take their time figuring out what direction they want to go. Even if you are applying to a program where you will not initially have an assigned supervisor, you should still be able to indicate at the time of application which faculty member you expect to end up with as a primary supervisor based on shared interests or orientations. Certain components of your application should be aimed at this *expected* supervisor. The importance of targeting specific graduate faculty members in the programs that you apply to will be revisited frequently over the next few chapters as we discuss different aspects of the application materials and procedures.

Finding someone who shares your research interests   If you are applying to a program that asks you to select your graduate supervisor, then you will indicate at the time of application who you would prefer. This means that first you will need to do some research that focuses on individual faculty. Look for recent publications (books, journal articles, etc.) in your field to find out who is doing what, and where they are doing it. When you are talking to your favorite professor about graduate school, ask whether he or she has colleagues at other universities who do work is in an area that interests you.

Many students fail to see the benefits of focusing on the prospective supervisor when considering where to apply to graduate school. It is more common for students to focus mainly on a school's general reputation, and only later do they begin to consider who they would like to study and work with. This is actually a somewhat backwards approach, and it can seriously hamper efforts to put together a good application package.

There are good reasons why it may be better to begin your selection of graduate programs by looking at the individual faculty members who are there and what their current research involves. First, the current interests of your supervisor will play the most significant role in determining precisely what you end up studying in graduate school — maybe not the courses you take, but definitely the nature of your thesis and other research. You need to know whether a prospective supervisor's interests are compatible with your own. Otherwise, you could end up somewhere that you would rather not be, studying something that you would rather not be studying, doing research that you would rather not be doing, or working with someone whom you would rather not be working with.

Second, you need to know what your prospective supervisors are currently interested in before you can write an effective personal statement, as you will need to demonstrate the appropriateness of the match between you and them. We will return to this issue in chapters

7 and 8. This same consideration applies to any cover letter that you might include with an initial preapplication contact with a prospective supervisor (see chapter 9).

The package of application materials you receive from a graduate program will sometimes include a list of the faculty members in the department and a description of their research, if applicable. As a note of caution, you should not assume that these statements of research interests are up-to-date. Professors' research interests and activities change from time to time, sometimes frequently, and sometimes the information in the application package is outdated and misleading. Later, we will discuss ways to make sure that you are up-to-date on your prospective supervisor's research interests and plans.

You should not put all your eggs in one basket by applying to only one graduate program. Because you want to find more than one program suitable to your goals, this means that you will also need to find more than one suitable prospective supervisor. This is another time when you want to talk to as many people in *your* department as possible, including the graduate students if there are any. The graduate students may tell you how they approached the task of choosing a supervisor and what kinds of pitfalls they encountered.

> *Students who are already in graduate school can give you invaluable insight into what it is really like. Ironically, they do not always give expert advice on how to get into a graduate program. That is because many of them don't really understand all the factors that led to their own admission to graduate school!*

Important factors beyond shared interests   Finding someone with research interests that are compatible with your own is the easiest part of finding an appropriate graduate supervisor. There are several other factors that you must consider. It might not be necessary to visit a graduate school in order to find out about the current research interests of its faculty members, but such a visit will be your best opportunity to ascertain whether any of the faculty members there are right or wrong for you in other ways.

One important thing to consider is interpersonal compatibility. It is exceedingly important that your supervisor is someone you can get along with. Few things are more miserable than working with someone you dislike! Even worse, many new graduate students quit their studies during their first year, or else they decide to change supervisors part way through the program, which can increase the total time to graduation. These choices are made for a variety of reasons, but they often stem from incompatibility between the supervisor and student.

There is only so much that you can get to know about someone from a short visit, but you need to get some idea of whether you and your supervisor can get along. Use your intuition. When you meet this person, do you like him or her, or is the first impression a negative one? The graduate students who are already in the program may be forthcoming with information about the faculty members there, including who is well liked and respected and who is not.

Before you decide on a prospective supervisor, try to find out whether there is a history of students under this person's supervision leaving the program without finishing, or else changing supervisors part way through. This might not be easy to ascertain. After all, you can't exactly ask professors directly whether their previous graduate students were happy with the student/supervisor relationship. You might, however, be able to ask a graduate student who has already been in the program for a while.

Even after you find a program that offers the degree you need and the specialization that you want, a faculty member in that program who has research interests that match your own, who is willing to supervise your thesis research, and whom you like, there are *still* things you should consider before making a commitment!

The quality and success of the research that you do in graduate school will depend on the ability of your supervisor to provide you with what you need, not only in terms of wisdom, moral support, and guidance, but also in terms of physical and other resources. Ask yourself the following questions about the prospective supervisor: Is this person well-known in his or her field? This is relevant, not because you will necessarily receive better training from someone who is well-known, but because you will likely want to become well-known yourself. The most straightforward way to accomplish this is by meeting important researchers or professionals in your field through your supervisor's network of friends, colleagues, and contacts.

Have the prospective supervisor's former graduate students gone on to have successful careers? Many factors determine the career success of an individual, only a few of which are influenced by the person's graduate supervisor. However, with faculty members who have been around for many years and who have supervised many graduate students, meaningful patterns can begin to emerge.

Is the prospective supervisor's research well-funded? You are going somewhere where you will be trained to do research or some other kind of scholarly work by someone who does this type of work for a living. Some types of research are expensive and only a well-funded supervisor will be able to provide you with the resources necessary for your training. It is irresponsible for someone without adequate funding to accept a graduate student, but it does happen. Students who are already in the program will be able to give you their informed opinions about the adequacy of the resources and facilities for research or other activities. (This may be less of an issue in some fields in which it is relatively inexpensive to conduct research).

You have to be concerned about more than just whether the prospective supervisor has funding now. You also need some kind of assurance that funding will likely be in place for the next few years, since that is the period over which you would be this person's student and perhaps at least partially dependent on his or her financial support. This might be difficult to determine, as it would be inappropriate to directly ask individuals about the number or size of their grants.

If you do not have the kind of experience needed to answer these questions for yourself, ask someone who does. Talk about these issues with your professors and with graduate students in your department, especially the more senior students who have been around for a couple of years or more. They might be able to give you some tips on estimating the quality of a prospective supervisor's capacity for supporting your graduate work.

The foregoing considerations — how well-known prospective supervisors are, how well-funded they are, and the career success of their former graduate students — would seldom be sufficient to indicate, when considered in isolation, whether an individual is a good or bad choice for a graduate supervisor. I have mentioned them here because they can be included in the whole mix of factors that you use to reach this decision. They may in fact become deciding factors if you end up in the enviable position of having offers from more than one program and you have to choose which one to accept.

Consider the pros and cons of selecting a supervisor who is newer or one more established in his or her field. Newer faculty members may be able to spend more time with you, since they will probably have fewer graduate students. On the other hand, their funding or tenure prospects may be more tenuous. Younger and newer faculty members are usually more "enthusiastic," sometimes owing in part to their desire to attain tenure. This enthusiasm can rub off on the students and help make their work more enjoyable. On the other hand, newer faculty members may not yet have an established reputation within their field that can help their students further down the road.

Older, more experienced faculty members may not be able to spend much time with you, or they may have more graduate students to handle. On the other hand, their funding may be more secure. They may be well-known and have a reputation that can help you, and they may have a network of colleagues within the field that you can eventually join.

What kind of working relationship are you looking for in a supervisor? Do you want someone looking over your shoulder or do you prefer to work more independently? Again, talk to the prospective supervisor's current graduate students to find out about the style of supervision.

Someone with general research interests that match your own may still be a poor match if there are specific and unavoidable features of their work for which you have a particular distaste. An Honors student whom I knew graduated with outstanding grades and with ample research experience in her general area of interest. She was a very likable person with many talents and credentials. She found a graduate program that was an excellent match for her objectives and her personality, and she sought to do her graduate work there under the supervision of a faculty member whose research focused on exactly the types of questions that interested her. Meanwhile, this faculty member happened to be looking for an able and eager student who shared those interests.

Everything seemed like a perfect match. That is, until the student discovered one critical detail about the prospective supervisor's program of research — all his experiments were highly computerized, and the student was technophobic. She knew absolutely nothing about computers, and was extremely anxious about having to learn even the basics. Although a graduate student working in this laboratory would not necessarily need to have an extensive background in computers, they would need at least a basic understanding and a willingness to learn some advanced concepts and applications. In the end, the professor decided that accepting this student was too much of a gamble, there was a high probability she would struggle through graduate school in his lab. I believe that she had already come to the same conclusion.

Summary   In most fields, a doctoral student's graduate work is done under the supervision of a particular faculty member; this is also true for master's students in many fields. If you will be applying to graduate programs where you would have a graduate supervisor, you may be expected to indicate who you would like this to be at the time of application. Making the right choices will require considerable advance research.

Researching prospective supervisors is similar in many respects to the task of researching graduate programs, with the main exception being that you will now focus on the specific expertise and interests of individual faculty members. There are two main reasons why you need to know who is who and what they do: First, the nature of your own graduate work will be partly determined by the nature of your supervisor's work. Second, you need to know what your prospective supervisor's needs are so that you can address them at various points in the application process.

Find out who is doing what, and where they are doing it, by browsing through recent books, journal articles, essays, etc., in your field of interest. Talk to your professors about your interests in graduate work. They may know people at other universities whose work is in an area that interests you. Use the Internet; many graduate programs have sites where you can find information about the research interests of its faculty members.

Other important factors beyond shared interests should be considered when selecting prospective supervisors. One of the most important is interpersonal compatibility; it can be a miserable tenure as a graduate student working under the guidance and supervision of someone you don't like. The best way to estimate what prospective supervisors are like on a personal level is to visit them in person, or talk with them on the telephone.

Other things that may be worth considering about prospective supervisors include: whether they are newer or more established, how well-known and how well-funded they are, and the career success of their former graduate students. You may also wish to know about an individual's style of supervising his or her graduate students.

You may be able to learn a great deal about individual faculty members by talking with graduate students who are currently in the program, either when you are visiting the program in person, or by telephone or electronic mail.

Do not neglect to discuss your plans for graduate work with your current professors. They are likely to be your best source of valuable tips and advice about selecting prospective graduate programs and supervisors.

The importance of choosing the right program, and when applicable, the right graduate supervisor, means that you should first establish at least general career objectives or research interests. Once you have done so, you will need to learn as much as you can about the programs that are available and the faculty members in those programs so that you can make the right choices.

II. How To Prepare An Application That Will Beat the Competition

You now have a good understanding of how the process of selecting graduate and professional school applicants generally works. The rest of this book is devoted to showing you how to improve your chances of getting into the right program.

Most students, whether they have mediocre grades or excellent grades, experience confusion and anxiety about applying to graduate school. Many fear that they will not succeed. You will soon know what to do and why you need to do it. The confusion and fear will go away, and you will be ready to proceed with confidence in devising and implementing a plan for getting into graduate school — perhaps into one of the best programs in your field.

In the chapters that follow, specific steps are recommended to strengthen each component of your application. There are some powerful strategies that you can use to improve the odds in your favor.

Many students who fail to get into graduate school will not apply again the following year. Their decision to give up so easily probably indicates that they lack the necessary determination for success in graduate school anyway.

Chapter 5

Applying Successfully With or Without Excellent Grades

Some Easy Ways To Improve the Odds

One suggestion that you will hear often is, "Apply to more than just one school!" You should definitely follow this advice. By now, you should be starting to understand why it is important to apply to several programs.

The key reasons have to do with how the selection process works. The decisions of admissions committees and graduate supervisors are products of human judgment, based on the consideration of several factors, both objective and subjective. With so much subjectivity in the process, there is no way of knowing whether you will be successful in striking the fancy of any particular group of admission committee members. In many cases, the prospective supervisor is the one who ultimately decides on the application, and there could be any one of several possible reasons why that person might not accept any particular applicant.

The point is that getting into graduate school can be capricious even for the students with really good grades. No students should take it for granted that they will be accepted into any particular program.

Although you would be wise to apply to more than one program, there is no advantage in applying to a large number of indiscriminately chosen programs. You will not improve the odds if you are unrealistic about which programs you apply to. Choices must be made on the basis of your research into what each of them has to offer, how well they match your interests and goals, how competitive they are, and how your own credentials (including grades) are likely to stack up against the competition.

Students with weak grades and mediocre standardized test scores, and who come from small and less prestigious undergraduate colleges, may not have much chance of getting into one of the more competitive and high-profile programs in their field. Applying to several such programs will just lead to more rejection letters and a bigger blow to the student's self-esteem. It might not be worth the time and effort, or the application fees, for such students to apply to these programs. But there are dozens of other programs for which their application might be quite competitive. If you do the kind of research that was suggested in chapter 4, then you should have little problem figuring out which programs are realistic for you, in light of your qualifications and the competitiveness of the various programs.

A similar consideration applies to students applying to programs in which they compete with others to have a particular faculty member agree to supervise their graduate studies. In general, the more well-known and highly regarded the prospective supervisor is in their field, the more highly qualified students there are likely to be applying to work with them each year. This stacks the deck against the students who have less sterling credentials. It is important to remember that although there may be some advantages to having a graduate supervisor who is highly accomplished and well known, this does not necessarily mean that he or she will be a better supervisor than someone who is less known. In fact, some brilliant researchers and scholars make lousy graduate supervisors. They often have more distractions that limit the amount of time they can spend with their graduate students.

How many programs should you apply to?   There is no simple answer to this question, as it depends on several factors. One factor to consider is the cost. For each application, you will have to pay for transcripts, standardized test scores, postage, and probably a nonrefundable application fee, which is typically in the range of $30 to $50. For some programs the application fees are considerably higher. You will need to follow up on each of your applications to make sure that all the materials have arrived (this topic is covered in detail in chapter 9). This may involve long-distance phone calls, the costs of which can quickly add up.

Although it is generally advisable that students do not choose potential programs based on the tuition or other costs associated with being a student there, this is a different issue, because paying for an education is one of the best personal investments you can make. By contrast, you are just wasting money by applying to more than a reasonable number of programs, or to only programs that you are clearly unlikely to get into.

There is also a limit to how much you can improve your chances of being accepted by simply increasing the number of programs you apply to. As you first increase the number of applications, the odds of being accepted into a suitable program increase accordingly. However, the law of diminishing returns begins to set in at some point. If you apply to too many programs, you may not be able to spend enough time on any one of the applications, and you will probably end up with some applications that fall short of the quality that could have been there.

Consider, for example, the quality of your personal statements or essays. The most effective ones will be somewhat customized for each particular program. How likely are you to do the best possible job of this with two dozen statements or essays? Even properly filling out an application form can take a lot of time. Thus, applying to too many programs can actually *decrease* your chances of getting into graduate school.

You also have to consider the amount of time your referees will be able to spend writing your letters of recommendation and filling out recommendation forms. If there are substantial differences among the programs you are applying to in terms of their focus areas, then you want your referees to be able to write letters that are somewhat customized to suit each program. It might be easy enough to ask for a small number of letters, but asking a busy professor to write two dozen letters will likely just get you two dozen short and ineffective letters, if it gets you any at all. Your referees might politely reassure you that they don't mind filling out your recommendation forms, but I can assure you that this is rarely a pleasure, and more often a chore. You do not want to impose more than a few recommendation forms on any one person.

Although several caveats have been noted, we have not really discussed how many programs you should apply to. That is because this decision should really be made by you, and will depend on your chosen field and on other circumstances. As a general guideline, you should probably be applying to at least four or five different programs *that you are well-qualified for,* and probably no more than ten or twelve. If you are applying to the competitive professional-degree programs, then you might want to apply to a few more.

A General Strategy for a Winning Application

It is important to remember that applying to graduate school is a competition between you and the other applicants to the same program. If you have a mediocre GPA, you are starting out at a disadvantage to those applicants with very good or outstanding GPAs. One aim of this book is to show you how you can overcome this disadvantage and actually obtain your own advantages.

Now that you know how the selection process works in most cases, you can appreciate the true nature of the competition. The competition is for the positive regard of the prospective supervisor or a few people on an admissions committee, and GPA is only one of several factors that will determine which applicants win. Some programs receive hundreds of applications each year, whereas others receive only a handful. Successful applicants usually do several things that the unsuccessful applicants don't do, and they often avoid making some of the same mistakes.

Most students submit all of the required components of their application (i.e., transcripts, standardized test scores, a personal statement, letters of recommendation, application fee, etc.) and then sit back and hope for the best. The success of their application is now in the hands of others — the individuals on the admissions committee and/or the prospective graduate supervisor — people who are strangers, and therefore, who know very little about the individual applicants and care even less about them.

By now, you should be starting to realize the foolishness of such complacency. You will soon know what to do differently, realizing that how well your application fares depends on the extra care you put into it and the extra measures you take. You will be able to proceed with confidence.

REMEMBER THIS IMPORTANT RULE

If you are trying to overcome a weak GPA, don't approach the application process in the same way as the majority of graduate school applicants. You must do some things differently, and you must do most things better. Lucky for you, most students don't have a very good idea of what they are doing when they apply to graduate school. They are unaware of their mistakes. With a little bit of insight, you can do better.

Aim from the outset to set yourself apart from the other applicants with whom you are competing. You can accomplish this by making your application unique, which does not mean being strange or bizarre. It means rising above the mediocrity of the typical applicants, even when your qualifications are not really any better.

The Importance of Relevant Experience

Applying to graduate school is, in many respects, like applying for a job. Anyone who has ever applied for a job knows the importance of having previous experience in the same or a similar kind of work. It is not impossible to get a job without previous experience — it's just much harder to do so. All other things being equal, most jobs will go to applicants with suitable experience.

Most students recognize the importance of getting relevant experience in research or fieldwork prior to applying to graduate school. Indeed, relevant experience is one of the most important of the nonobjective criteria that admissions committees and prospective supervisors assess in graduate school applicants. For some programs it is virtually a requirement. Like job applicants, graduate school applicants who already have some practical experience in their field are more likely to perform well because of the knowledge and skills they possess.

From the point of view of both the employer and the graduate admissions committee, the experienced applicants have a lower risk of failure because they have previously demonstrated an ability to do the kinds of work that will be required of them on the job or in graduate school. The main advantage to the prospective employer is that the experienced applicant will require less training than a naive one, thus saving the employer time and money. Similarly, graduate schools benefit from savings in the cost of administering their programs when their students perform well and earn their degrees in a timely fashion.

Job applicants, for the most part, will usually benefit from having previous experience only if this experience also serves to benefit the prospective employer. By contrast, there are many additional and direct benefits to the student who obtains as much relevant experience as possible prior to applying to graduate school. First, such experience often gives students an opportunity to find out in advance what a career in their field of interest might be like. If the experience is not enjoyable, students can save themselves from years of training for a career they would ultimately dislike. If the experience is enjoyable, a student might become even more focussed and determined to pursue a career in that field. This determination will serve them well in graduate school.

As we will discuss later on, getting relevant experience is also essential to lining up the best letters of recommendation and for writing an effective personal statement for your graduate-school application. From the point of view of an admissions committee or prospective supervisor, the student who has sought out relevant work experience has already demonstrated the kind of initiative and interest in their field they will need to be a successful graduate student.

Of course, there are some areas of graduate study and research for which there are no obvious ways for an undergraduate student to get preparatory experience outside of a classroom. For instance, it is hard to imagine how a Mathematics student could get involved in original research in his or her field before first taking several semesters of advanced classes at the graduate level. One could list other examples, but the real problem is that students often fail to realize the number of ways there are to get the experience they need for graduate school.

This is an area where an undergraduate advisor might be able to help you if this person can tell you how students in your department typically obtain relevant experience. The advisor will be able to tell you what classes require students to work on a research project for course credit, or whether there is an opportunity for you to do an independent study. The advisor might also be able to tell you what kinds of off-campus employment or volunteer opportunities exist in your locale, or they might be able to direct you to someone who can provide you with this type of information.

> *Research or other relevant work-experience opportunities for undergraduates do not exist in all fields. For example, the "vertical" nature of some sciences, like Mathematics or Physics, requires that students first obtain a working knowledge of fundamentally complex subject matter before they could ever hope to participate in original research. Academic performance (i.e., grades) tends to be weighted more heavily in the evaluation of applicants to programs in these fields.*

It is common in some departments for professors to hire students to work as part-time or full-time research assistants and pay them from a research grant. If you ask, an advisor will probably be able to tell you which faculty members in your department tend to provide such opportunities to students. Ask other students in the department if they know anything about such opportunities. Check departmental bulletin boards for help-wanted ads.

Find out if your school runs a work-study program. These are usually government-sponsored programs designed to share the cost of employing students in relevant work, often with faculty members in certain departments who can provide such opportunities. Many work-study programs are intended only for financially needy students, so not everyone is eligible.

Don't be shy about seeking opportunities to gain essential experience. There is nothing wrong with approaching professors and asking if they need a volunteer research assistant. You might get a pleasant surprise. Some professors never solicit students to help them with their research, but instead wait until volunteers come knocking at their door. Look for job opportunities and volunteer opportunities off campus, too.

If you do get hired for either paid or volunteer work, be willing to make a commitment and put in sufficient time and effort so that you will actually be of benefit to your employer or supervisor, and to their work. A mistake that some students make is to volunteer to help out for only a few hours each week, and in some such cases, once the time and effort required to train them is taken into account, the arrangement proves not to be beneficial to the person whom they were intending to help. Someone who does not see you as having helped is not likely to write a strong letter of recommendation on your behalf.

Begin looking for opportunities early   Although most students who are serious about graduate school eventually realize the importance of getting relevant work experience related to their field, the majority of them fail to take measures to get such experience until it is too late to take full advantage of the best opportunities available. A good time to begin trying to find relevant work experience in your field is in the second semester of your sophomore year or during your junior year.

One reason for looking for these opportunities as early as possible is that you might not end up with something immediately. Perhaps you wish to work as a volunteer research assistant in the laboratory of one of your professors, but when you ask her about it she regretfully tells you that her lab is already full and she really doesn't have anything for you to do. She may suggest, however, that you come by and ask again at the end of the semester, or perhaps next year.

Another reason to look for work-experience opportunities as early as possible is that you might be fortunate to find something now, and also to find other relevant work doing something slightly different, or working with someone different next year. This way you would end up getting even more experience to cite later on in your personal statement and another good letter of recommendation from someone who can speak to your potential as a graduate student.

Do not be overly alarmed if you are already in your senior year and you realize that you still do not have any work experience or other practical experience in your field. You might still have time. But it is important that you immediately move this objective to the top of your priority list before it really does become too late.

> *Summer is the best time to find employment or volunteer opportunities as a professor's assistant. Many students think their professors work five days a week during the academic year and take the summer off. For many professors, being free from having to deliver lectures and grade papers during the summer means they can spend more time on their research. This is when they are most in need of students' help.*

Other kinds of relevant experience   There are other kinds of experience related to your field of study that you can acquire in addition to work experience. Whether you are in your freshman or senior year, you should make a habit of attending events hosted by your department, such as talks or colloquia by invited guests. Check the bulletin boards in your department every week to see what kinds of events are upcoming.

One straightforward reason for attending department-sponsored events or talks is that you will probably learn something interesting that you did not previously know, and it might even be something that helps you in one or more of your classes. You might also gain insight into some of the things that specialists in your field do, the kinds of careers or research that you might someday be involved in yourself. Perhaps you will discover that you would like to pursue an academic career like that enjoyed by some of your professors.

After a while, the faculty who attend these events will get

used to seeing you around and will view you as a committed and dedicated student who has intrinsic interest in the field. Your attendance at such events will allow you to learn more about the professors in your department, which may eventually provide opportunities to get to know some of them personally, thus providing the basis for a future letter of recommendation. This is one way to begin feeling like you are part of your department.

At the same time, you should be trying to learn as much as you can about the faculty in your department, what their research is about, what courses they teach, etc. It takes a while to get this sort of intimate knowledge of your department, so begin pursuing it while you are still in your sophomore year, if not earlier. If you are in your freshman or sophomore year, one of the easiest ways to find out who-is-who in your department is by talking to juniors and seniors who have had more experience with a greater number of the professors, and who are likely to be better acquainted with the curriculum.

Summary   In many graduate programs, relevant work-experience is one of the most important nonobjective criteria by which admissions committees and faculty rate applicants. In any given year there will be some applicants who have various amounts of relevant experience and some who have none at all. The latter applicants are less likely to be selected.

Relevant experience can be gained in many ways and the types of opportunities that exist will vary across disciplines. Options for obtaining relevant experience can be straightforward in departments in which faculty are engaged in ongoing research. Working as a research assistant will give you invaluable experience, which will be of potential benefit in several ways. It may be your first close-up look at the kind of career that will be possible after obtaining an advanced degree. Working for a professor is also the best way to set yourself up for a good letter of recommendation later on.

If there is still time for you to do so prior to applying to graduate school, try to get relevant experience from more than one place under the supervision of more than one potential future referee for your letters of recommendation.

Try to get "connected" with your department by showing up at talks and other department-sponsored events. Get to know the faculty members, and allow them to get to know you. Professors can be powerful people. They can have a great deal to do with your success or failure in applying to graduate school. You need their support, but you won't get it if they don't know who you are.

> *Most universities have some kind of mentor program, usually run by the alumni association or student placement services. These programs match students with alumni who rely on their personal and professional experience to advise students on possible career options and on the realities of the workplace. The student may be allowed to spend some time observing or even helping the mentor on the job.*

Some advisors recommend that prospective graduate students apply to at least two or three programs that fit their interests. I recommend about twice that many for most students. This will allow you to apply to a balance of program types. For example, you may wish to set your goals high and apply to one or two highly competitive research programs, while also taking a more conservative approach and applying to a couple of schools with large graduate programs where you would have a better chance of getting in, and one or two programs that fit your academic needs and that are almost certain to accept you. This way you are more certain to get in somewhere. All the better if it is in one of the top programs.

Chapter 6

Enhancing the Objective Components of Your Application

How do graduate admissions committees decide who is acceptable for their programs? One common misconception is that the only important components of a graduate school application are the quality of the students grades and standardized test scores. This is not true at all! The letters of recommendation and the applicant's personal statement or essays are also very important. They are often the difference between a successful application and an unsuccessful one. Even the way an application form is filled out can make a difference.

The various people looking at your application may differ in how they weigh its assorted components. Therefore, you should pay close attention to each one of them. At the same time, keep in mind that few applicants achieve excellence on all of the important dimensions, so you should not be discouraged if you think you come up a bit short on one or two of them. If you make selective and appropriate use of the information and advice in this book, you should do fine.

Some shortcomings are easier to overcome than others. For example, if you lack work or research experience in your area, or other relevant background, you can probably correct that. On the other hand, if you have already written your standardized tests and obtained poor scores, there is nothing you can do to erase them completely from your record. Likewise, there is little you can do to hide poor grades that appear on your transcripts. By contrast, you still have plenty of time to arrange for good letters of recommendation and to prepare an effective personal statement. And as you will see, there is a multitude of other things that you can do to make yourself an attractive candidate. Do not worry about things you can do nothing about. Optimize what you can — it might make up for any irreversible weaknesses.

The next two chapters deal with the five common components of most graduate or professional school applications — application forms, official transcripts of all college or university courses you have taken and the grades you obtained, standardized test scores, letters of recommendation, and the personal statement, essay, or essays. There is a major section devoted to each of these, explaining how they are used by admissions committees and prospective supervisors, and how you can enhance their quality in your own application.

This chapter deals with the objective components of your application — your transcripts and standardized test scores. In the last section of this chapter, we will discuss the pitfalls of filling out application forms and how to do it right. Chapter 7 deals with the nonobjective elements of the application, including the personal statement and letters of recommendation, and also the preselection interviews that are administered by some programs.

Undergraduate Grades and Coursework

Something emphasized throughout this book is that many students can overcome a less-than-outstanding GPA and still get into graduate school. But it has also been repeatedly acknowledged that students' chances of success are better if they do have excellent grades. Unless you are in your final semester of your senior year, there is still time to improve your grades and thereby enhance your graduate school prospects. I won't insult your common sense by suggesting that you study harder. You have already thought of that. There are reasons why you have the GPA that you have, and only you know what those reasons are. Only you know whether it is possible for you to work harder than you already do.

Not all equal grades are equal   One of the problems with discriminating between applicants on the basis of their GPAs is that it is not always clear what a particular GPA actually means about a student's academic ability. For instance, suppose that student A graduated from college A and student B graduated from college B. They took similar undergraduate courses and their GPAs are exactly the same. Does this mean that their academic performances were equal? No, of course it doesn't. They didn't take exactly the same courses with the same professors — they didn't even go to the same school. Every student knows that some professors tend to give higher grades than others, and that certain courses are much harder than others. Admissions committees know this too, and that is one reason why they look beyond the simple numeric value of a GPA to determine an applicant's academic credentials. Still, you can count on your GPA being the *first* thing that is looked at when you are compared to other applicants.

The extent to which undergraduate GPA is a good predictor of graduate school performance depends upon the field of study and on the relative emphasis that a particular program places on course work as a degree requirement. However, all programs that involve course work will have some interest in an applicant's GPA. After all, students have to pass their graduate courses before they can earn their graduate degree. Most students assume that graduate courses are significantly more difficult than undergraduate courses. In fact, many students are pleasantly surprised to discover that their graduate courses are actually easier!

Before you get too despondent over your less-than-stellar GPA, ask yourself the following questions about your record: Did you get most of your poor grades in your freshman and sophomore years? Have your grades improved in more recent semesters? What would your GPA look like if you could exclude the grades from your first few semesters? Many programs place more emphasis on the grades from the most recent undergraduate years, and give only secondary consideration to the first year or two. This should give you hope if you are not yet in your senior year and so far have obtained only mediocre grades. You may still have a chance to do better in the courses that count the most.

In some disciplines, there are certain undergraduate courses that are especially important if you are planning on continuing into graduate school. Some programs may look closely to see whether you have taken these courses and what grades you obtained in them. These grades may be weighed more heavily than the grades in your other courses. Most students figure out what courses are the most important in their field of study before they get too far into their undergraduate program, and in many instances these courses are compulsory for any specializing student. But there may be other important courses that are less obvious. Find out what they are by asking an undergraduate advisor or one of your professors. The earlier you find out which are the most significant courses, the less likely you are to graduate without having taken them. When you do enrol in one of these key courses, put everything you can into it and strive for a top grade.

Other options for bolstering your grades and coursework   If you are in your senior year, there may not be time to do much about your grades before you graduate. There are, however, a few ideas that you might consider. One option is to do an unclassified year of undergraduate study to improve your GPA. You might take some of those special courses that are preferred by graduate programs in your field, if you haven't already taken them, or if you have taken them and obtained less than a B+. Although this will delay graduation by a few months, it will also demonstrate your determination and the seriousness of your intentions for graduate school.

It may be possible to do a qualifying year of study at the university to which you are applying for graduate school. Some programs may not accept certain applicants unconditionally, but instead invite them to enrol in select undergraduate courses for one or more semesters with the intention of formally accepting them into the graduate program if they do well. Other possibilities might exist. Get on the phone and ask the Graduate Program Director if you are concerned about being rejected solely on the basis of your grades.

> *Many students are able to improve their GPA by letting professors know they are committed to improving their academic record to get into graduate school. Sometimes this is all it takes to get extra tutoring needed to master the subject matter of a particular course.*

Summary   Admissions committees and other graduate program faculty members understand that two grades of equal numeric value do not necessarily reflect equivalent academic achievement. This is one reason why they often consider the specific courses that applicants have taken.

In most disciplines, there are certain courses that all graduate school applicants are expected to have taken. The grades they obtain in these courses may be more heavily weighted than their other grades. If you are not sure what the key courses are in your field of study, ask an undergraduate advisor or one of your professors.

Many programs will look for evidence of improving academic performance over the course of an applicant's undergraduate program. Admissions committees often weigh a student's grades for the final two years of undergraduate training somewhat more heavily than the grades from the first two years.

Even if you are in your senior year, it might not be too late to bolster your grades. Students who graduate with disappointing grades may consider taking an unclassified year of undergraduate study. Some graduate programs may invite applicants to take a "qualifying" year of study, in which the student has to take specific courses and do well in them.

Standardized Tests

Scores on standardized tests constitute the second objective criterion (undergraduate GPA was the first) on which applicants to graduate or professional degree programs are evaluated. The easiest way to find out which test(s) you will likely need to write is to ask one of your professors, or go and look through the program guides in the reference section of your library or on the Internet. Brief descriptions of some common tests follow.

The nature and purpose of standardized tests   If you think you are doomed to do poorly on these standardized tests because you obtain only mediocre grades in your college or university classes, then think again. In many cases, there is little relation between one's GPA and their scores on standardized tests, which are primarily aptitude tests. As with most tests that you have written in the past, performance on the standardized tests depends more on how well-prepared you are than on how smart you are. But don't be fooled. It takes a long time to properly prepare for these tests, so you should begin early.

Most applicants to graduate programs in the arts and sciences are required to take the Graduate Record Examination (GRE). For some Psychology programs applicants must write the Millers Analogies Test (MAT). If you want to go to a school of Business or Management you will probably have to take the Graduate Management Admissions Test (GMAT). For admission into medical school, you will have to take the Medical College Admissions Test (MCAT). International applicants from non-English speaking countries will probably have to pass the Test of English as a Foreign Language (TOEFL). Some of the other common standardized tests include:

LSAT - Law School Admissions Test

VCAT - Veterinary College Admissions Test

DAT - Dental Admissions Test   (U.S.)
       Dental Aptitude Test   (Canada)

When to take the tests   It is important that you find out which tests you will have to take long before you expect to be applying to graduate school. There are several reasons why: First, most standardized tests are administered on only a few (e.g., four or five) specific days of the year. The date that you take the test is important. It must be early enough that your results can be processed and mailed to the programs that you are applying to by their application deadlines. It takes about six weeks for the testing service to process and send out your official scores. You need to find out about the test dates and locations and your graduate school application deadlines early enough so that you can plan accordingly.

A common mistake is to begin planning for standardized tests too late to enable oneself to take the tests on the necessary test dates, and without enough time to fully prepare for the tests. Many students end up doing poorly because of their lack of preparation, or else they end up delaying their application to graduate studies by a year. Do not make this mistake yourself.

You must register in advance, usually a minimum of five weeks prior to the date that you wish to take the test, and you will have to pay a nominal fee. You can make arrangements to write some tests on less than five weeks notice if you are willing to pay a late registration fee. The MCAT and LSAT are among those for which there is a chance of late registration; however, there is no late registration for the GRE, and late registration for the GMAT is currently only available at U.S. centres. Another possibility is stand-by registration on the day of the test. You have to show up, but there is no guarantee that you will get to take the test.

In addition to the paper and pencil versions of these tests, some of them are now available in a computerized format and can be written almost anytime during the year. The fee to write the computerized versions is higher than for the pencil and paper versions.

Most colleges and universities have testing centers where the tests are administered, but depending on where you live it is also possible that you will have to travel a great distance to reach the nearest testing center. Space is limited and so are the dates on which the tests can be taken, so you should register early — it will improve your chances of being assigned to your first choice of testing centers and dates.

Let's look at an example that shows the importance of making arrangements to take these tests well in advance of the graduate program application deadlines. Suppose the deadline for application to a graduate program is mid-January (a common deadline), and you have to take the GRE. In the present example, you will need to write the test no later than on the October test date. The December date will not do because it takes another five to six weeks after you take the test for the Educational Testing Service to process your scores and mail them out. If you write the test in October, your scores will be sent by early December and the graduate schools to which you are applying will receive them in time for their mid-January application deadlines. If you do not take the GRE until the December test date, then your scores will not be sent out until the end of January, thus missing the application deadline.

In order to have your scores sent to the graduate program on time, you will need to register for the GRE by the end of August (or earlier if you live outside the United States) because the Educational Testing Service must receive your registration materials five to six weeks before the test date. If you are reading this anytime after the beginning of September and you wish to write the test in October, you will probably have to apply to write the computerized version. Note that the computerized version is only available for the GRE General test; GRE Subject Tests are available in pencil and paper format only.

If for some reason you are not able to take the test in time to have your official scores sent to the graduate school by the application deadline, this might not disqualify your application. If, for example, you are not able to write until the December test date and you have a graduate school application deadline of mid-January, then you must contact the Graduate Program Director or secretary before the deadline and let them know that you have written the tests and that your official scores are on the way.

This won't work in all cases, because some graduate programs adhere strictly to their application deadlines and will not consider applications that are still incomplete after that date. Some programs might show a bit of leniency, but you should never put yourself in the position of needing it. It makes a much better impression to everyone who views your application file if it is complete when they see it for the first time. We will return to this issue in chapter 7.

The Educational Testing Service has recently been considering phasing out the October test date for the GRE. At the time of writing this edition, the October test date was still being offered. Check first before you plan to write the GRE in October.

Some people advise that, if possible, students should write the standardized tests at least a year in advance of graduate school application. The logic here is that if students do poorly on the tests, they will still have time to write them again with better preparation. This is reasonable advice in many instances, but writing the test early should not be done in lieu of proper preparation. Even if you do poorly and choose to rewrite the tests, you will not remove your poor first scores from your record. They will be shown along with the official scores you obtain the second time you take the tests.

Writing the tests well in advance of graduate school application gives you more time to prepare. When students write the tests at the latest possible date to enable the testing service to get the official scores out to the graduate programs before the application deadlines, this usually means that they are preparing for the tests at the same time that they are dealing with all of the other aspects of their applications. Meanwhile, they may also be immersed in a regular undergraduate course load. There is only so much time available to study for ongoing classes, solicit letters of recommendation, fill out application forms, write personal statements, and prepare for standardized tests. It is certain that something will be compromised.

There may even be a psychological advantage to writing tests early. Some people feel less pressure knowing that they have time to take them again if they have to. This may enhance test performance in some individuals by preventing anxiety or panic, thereby facilitating concentration.

One clear exception to the notion that one should write their standardized tests at least a year in advance of graduate school application applies to special subject tests of the GRE. It may be better in some instances to write the general test several months to a year prior to the application period, for reasons cited above, but to write the subject tests closer to the end of your undergraduate program. The main reason for delaying the writing of the subject tests is that much of the preparation for these tests actually comes from the undergraduate courses that you take in that subject. The more courses you have taken in a subject area the better prepared you should be for the GRE subject test. Writing the general and subject tests at different times should allow you more time to prepare for each one.

If you are reading this and do not have much time before you must write your standardized test(s), then at least consider the following advice: If you have to write more than one, try to write them at least a few weeks apart. Not only do you need the preparation time, but they are very gruelling tests and you will need some time to recover and clear your head following the first one.

How to get the information you need   Your current school should have an office that can provide you with all the information you need to register for whatever standardized tests you need to write. They should also be able to give you free publications that describe the characteristics and features of the tests, the test dates, the location of nearby test centers, registration procedures, and how to prepare for taking the tests.

The following are mailing addresses for details concerning registration, processing, and other important information for some common standardized tests:

Graduate Record Examinations
Educational Testing Service
P.O. Box 6000
Princeton, NJ
USA 08541-6000

MCAT Program Office
P.O. Box 4056
Iowa City, IA
USA 52243-4056

Graduate Management Admission Test
Educational Testing Service
P.O. Box 6103
Princeton, NJ
USA 08541-6103

How to prepare for the tests   Preparing for standardized tests is very different than for tests like the ones in your undergraduate courses. Most of the tests consist of a series of strictly timed sections. This puts a lot of pressure on the examinee. What is important to know is that there is a strong correlation between examinees' scores and how many questions in each section they are able to complete without guessing or running out of time. This might seem obvious, but it also suggests the best strategy for preparing. For instance, the best way to study for the GRE general test *is not* to read books and attempt to learn and retain massive amounts of information. The best way to prepare is to get as much practice as possible with the *types* of questions that are on the test.

The key to this strategy of preparing for the GRE is that there are only a few types of questions that appear on the test, and there are several questions of each type. The information embodied by specific questions will vary, but the way to approach solving many of them will be generally similar. If you prepare accordingly, your advantage over the other examinees will come from being able to solve questions quickly, without mistakes, and without having to spend as much time reading and interpreting the test instructions or questions.

Luckily, this advantage is easy to obtain if you are willing to put in the time and effort. There are several publications and practice tests that will help you prepare. These are available in most college bookstores, and in some off-campus retail bookstores. Take as many of these practice tests as you can prior to writing the real test. If you are reading this and you still have a few months before you will be writing the official test, you should try to write at least one practice test per week.

Over time, you should see a gradual improvement in your scores as you become more efficient at answering the types of questions on the test. If you have less time between now and the real test, you should take the practice tests more frequently, perhaps one every other day. Statistics indicate that there is a high degree of test-retest reliability on standardized tests, so your scores on the last few practice tests should provide a reasonable estimate of the scores you are likely to obtain on the official test.

In addition to reading preparation booklets and writing as many practice tests as you can, there are businesses you can go to that provide courses on preparing for standardized tests. Princeton Review and Kaplan's are two which advertise in college newspapers. One gimmick that Princeton Review uses is to offer a free full-length practice test under simulated testing conditions. Although this may be just a marketing ploy aimed at convincing you to enrol in their courses, which some would consider to be rather expensive, it may also be your best chance to get a good picture of exactly what to expect on the day of the real test.

Summary   Preparation is the key to successful performance on standardized tests, but most students don't begin their preparations far enough in advance to take full advantage. If possible, you should begin to take the following steps during the last semester of your junior year.

Your first step is to find out what standardized test(s) you will need to take in order to get into a graduate program in your field. Next, go to your college bookstore or the library and purchase or borrow books on preparing for the tests that you will need to write. Prepare for the tests by writing several practice tests, or register with a training service that offers courses on preparing for standardized tests.

Get information from your school on the test dates and the location of the nearest testing centers. Timing is critical. Remember that you must register to write these tests several weeks in advance of the test date. Moreover, it takes about six weeks after your test date for the testing service to process and mail out your official test scores. You will, therefore, need to arrange to write the tests well in advance of your earliest graduate program application deadline. If you choose to write the tests several months before applying to graduate school, remember that you will have to make arrangements with the testing service at least six weeks in advance of any application deadlines so that your official scores are received by the programs on time.

> *Students with weak grades can sometimes take advantage of the fact that minimum GPA requirements are usually somewhat lower for master's programs than for doctoral programs. It may be easier to get into the master's program now, and it will be easier to qualify for the doctoral program later once you have the master's degree. This strategy does not necessarily increase the amount of time it takes overall to obtain the doctorate.*

Application Forms

Filling out application forms is a straightforward step, right? Well, it should be. But if it is, then why do students make so many mistakes on this task? Two reasons account for most of the mistakes on application forms: First, most students mistakenly think that it only takes a couple of hours to fill out an application form, but it really takes much longer than that to do it properly. Second, many students are simply careless and fail to properly follow instructions. The consequences are usually forms that are messy, inaccurate, or incomplete. The quality of a completed application form contributes, like everything else, to the overall impression that an applicant makes.

Filling out application forms can be a tedious and frustrating task, but it is well worth the time and effort required to avoid making mistakes that leave a bad impression. Whether or not you believe that we can infer anything significant about people by the way they fill out application forms, some people do believe this and some of those people are on graduate admissions committees. It is easy to make mistakes when filling out application forms that diminish the good impressions you are trying to make. Fortunately, it is just as easy to avoid these mistakes if you know what to watch for.

Organization is the key   Most application packages have several items in them. These may include multiple application forms, return envelopes, evaluation forms for your referees; some packages also include special envelopes for your referees, confirmation-of-receipt postcards for you to fill out, and additional items that need to be dealt with in some way or another. There may be multiple addresses that various forms and other items need to be mailed to, and various deadlines. No two application packages are identical, and the more programs you are applying to the more chances there are for you to make a mistake. Put all of the materials that you receive from each program into a separate folder. Try to have only one set of application materials out of its folder at a time. This will help you to keep track of things and avoid misfiling.

Most graduate school applications involve two forms — one for the department you are applying to and another one that is used for all the graduate programs in the university. Carefully note where you are to send these forms; they may need to go to the same address, or different addresses. You will need to keep track of what you send, where you send it, and the date that you send it. We will return to the issue of organization and record keeping in chapter 9.

Make two photocopies of each form. You will spend most of your time working with these photocopies, and you will deal with the originals only after you have everything right on a practice version. Fill in all of the line items and check the appropriate boxes on the first copy. Work in pencil so that you can correct mistakes and do other editing as you go along. Once you are satisfied that this copy is complete and accurate, try typing in the information on the second copy (not the original, yet). The main purpose is to make sure you can get things to fit in the appropriate spaces on the forms. Some forms provide ridiculously tiny spaces, which can make things especially challenging for those of us with little or no typewriting skills. If it is not possible to type in a small item because the space provided is even smaller, try printing it neatly in black ink.

> *Avoid the stress of having to correct mistakes on the original form by first getting it right on a copy.*

Time needed for filling out forms   Most students mistakenly expect to spend a couple of hours, or only slightly more, filling out a graduate school application form. It can take much longer than that for some of the longer and more complicated ones. The first one might even take a couple of days to get right! That is, at least if you are doing a good job of it. The rest should go a bit quicker, perhaps only a few hours each, because some items will be used again or only slightly modified from those first forms, and with repeated practice, some aspects of filling out forms become acquired skills and you become more efficient.

Many of the line items on application forms are straightforward and the information is readily available, such as biographical data. Others require a bit more thought on exactly what to put down, such as relevant employment history, research experience, or work in progress. Think about what you are writing down for items like these. Consider how it would sound from the perspective of the admissions committee members. Take a little bit of extra time here — it can make a difference.

Provide complete and accurate information   Try to respond to every question and line item. An incomplete form suggests that the applicant is careless or lazy, and not very serious about getting into graduate school. If an item is not applicable, indicate this rather than leaving the line blank so it is clear that you have not merely overlooked that item.

When applicants fail to properly follow instructions for filling out the forms, it suggests that they either do not understand or do not respect simple instructions. If the precise meaning of a question or line item is not clear to you, then ask someone who is likely to be able to give you the proper interpretation. You may look foolish if you guess incorrectly at the intended meaning of an ambiguous item.

Although I emphasize throughout this book that there are some things that you should be doing differently than most other applicants, there are also some areas where it is critical that you conform to norms and expectations. This involves judgment. One area where conformity is important is in the appearance and order of your application materials. You are expected to fill out all sections of your application form. It is easier for admissions committee members to make direct comparisons between applicants if they have all submitted material in the same format. Do not simply attach a copy of your résumé and refer the reader to it when filling out an application form. Fill in all line items directly on the form.

There may be certain items on an application form that allow you to attach pages if the relevant information cannot fit inside the space on the form. You should minimize the number of attached sheets, using them only if you are certain that you cannot fit the information on the form. Do not, however, cram the information into the space on the form if it will look messy.

Neatness matters   A messy form suggests that the applicant is disorganized and sloppy. When it is difficult to read the items on a form, it suggests that the applicant is inconsiderate of those who must read the form.

After you fill out the practice forms that you have copied, check them over to make sure that there are no spelling or grammatical errors. Take your time when transferring information from your completed copies to the originals, and move your cup of coffee far away from your working area. If it is at all possible, complete all forms with a typewriter, using black ink. Make sure you are using a clean, new ribbon.

The task of dealing with application forms is just as tedious and boring for admissions committees as it is for the applicant. Avoid irritating these important decision makers with a messy, incomplete, or inaccurate form.

Double-check before you mail   Before you seal and mail the envelope, double check to make sure that everything is complete and accurate. You may feel so much relief and excitement at being done and ready to mail your application that you decide not to do this final check. That can be a costly decision. Even a single line item left blank can count against your application. Make sure you have signed the forms! A missing signature is not an easy problem to rectify. Have you enclosed (and signed) the check for any application fees? Double-check the mailing address for accuracy and legibility, and make sure that your return address is neat and easy to read.

Summary   The quality of a completed application form contributes to the overall impression that an applicant makes. Unfortunately, many students make mistakes while filling out application forms without realizing that they are doing anything wrong. There is more to properly filling out application forms than simply providing the right information.

Many students underestimate the time required to do a good job of filling out forms, and they end up sending forms that are messy, inaccurate, or incomplete. A messy form suggests that the applicant is disorganized and sloppy; an incomplete form suggests that the applicant is careless or lazy; an inaccurate form suggests that the applicant is unable to follow simple instructions.

Many programs will require that you fill out two slightly different forms, which you may have to send to different addresses. Organization is the key to keeping track of multiple forms. Make photocopies of your application forms and get everything right on these copies before transferring it all to the original forms.

Students should keep a folder containing all of the syllabi for courses they take during undergraduate school. This can be a precious time-saver later on if they ever need to provide details about their academic background.

Chapter 7

Enhancing the Nonobjective Components of Your Application

This chapter deals with the nonobjective elements of the application, including the personal statement, letters of recommendation, and the preselection interviews that are administered by some programs. There are considerable differences across disciplines, and across various programs within any given field, in terms of the relative importance of the objective and nonobjective components of a graduate school application.

The nonobjective measures often say more about the applicant as a *person*, and sometimes this is the most important information about an applicant. In many respects, these are the most difficult things about an application for the admissions committee to evaluate.

Importantly, these are also the areas where many students can make up for their mediocre grades or standardized test scores. Just as importantly, students who have excellent grades and test scores should understand that they may fail to get into graduate or professional school if any of the nonobjective components of their applications are particularly poor.

Letters of Recommendation

Most graduate programs require applicants to obtain from two to four letters of recommendation. The most common requirement is three. Some programs supply a special evaluation form, which the person writing the recommendation (hereafter referred to as the *referee*) is expected to complete, either in addition to or instead of a letter. Most programs ask for similar information.

The key to acquiring three good letters of recommendation is to start planning for them as soon as possible. Even if you need them in just a few weeks, there are still many things you can do to improve your chances of acquiring positive and effective letters. Start thinking about your letters of recommendation, now! It will make a big difference!

You must ask the right individuals to write letters for you, and you must request this favor in an appropriate fashion. This section explains: 1) how admissions committees and prospective graduate supervisors use letters of recommendation, 2) who you should ask for a letter of recommendation, 3) how to ensure that your referees write letters that actually help you, and 4) how to request a letter of recommendation.

A number of different terms may be used to refer to a person who writes a letter of recommendation, including *reference*, *recommender*, or *referee*. This book uses the term *referee*.

How are letters of recommendation used?   Unlike transcripts and standardized test scores, which are intended to provide objective measures of your scholarly aptitude, letters of recommendation provide more of a nonobjective evaluation of who you are, your important character traits, your abilities, and your potential for success in graduate school. Some of the people who will be deciding the fate of your application may be more interested in your letters of recommendation than any other component. In some cases, an excellent letter of recommendation can compensate for mediocre performance on the objective criteria such as GPA and standardized test scores.

On the other hand, it is sometimes argued that letters of recommendation are not very useful for discriminating between applicants because all letters are basically good, and so they have little impact on the outcome of the application. Whether or not the former is true, the latter certainly is not! A single statement in one letter of recommendation can sometimes make the difference between a successful graduate school application and an unsuccessful one.

It pays to think about the contents of your application from the point of view of the prospective supervisor or admissions committee members. After all, they are the people whose positive regard you need to win. Different individuals will be looking for slightly different things, but for the most part, the concerns of all those who read your letters of recommendation will be whether you have demonstrated to someone who is qualified to judge that you possess skills, aptitude, and character traits that are suited to graduate school in general, and to the specific objectives of their program.

Members of the admissions committee will look closely at your letters to determine whether your general aptitudes and interests are suited to their program. Prospective supervisors will look for similar insight into your suitability for their specific area of study or research. The admissions committee will be concerned with how well you are likely to perform as a student in their program. The prospective supervisor will want some indication that taking you on as their graduate student will be of mutual benefit to both of you.

Before deciding who to ask for a letter of recommendation, you need to appreciate the kinds of things that should be in a good recommendation. Most evaluation forms ask the referee how long they have known you, how well they know you, and in what capacity (e.g., as professor for one of your classes, your employer, your Honors thesis supervisor, etc.). They might be asked to describe the population to which you are being compared (e.g., All senior undergraduates in the department? The group of students who are enrolled in the Honors program this year? How many people are in this comparison group?), and to provide a global rating of your ability or potential in relation to that comparison population (e.g., would you be in the top 5%, the top 10%, top 25%, top 50%, bottom 50%?). The evaluation form might ask the referee whether your academic potential is fairly reflected in your grades.

> *Here is a simple way to see what kinds of things are on a typical evaluation form, even if it will be several months before you are applying to any programs: If you are currently at or near a university that has a graduate program in your field of interest, or in a related field, request the application package. If there is an evaluation form, you will see the kinds of questions that referees might need to answer about you when you apply to this program or to a similar one.*

Who would you ask if you needed three letters of recommendation right now? Some students find it difficult to come up with one or two marginally adequate choices, let alone three good ones. If you find that no one comes immediately to mind, just list the three faculty members in your school who best know you, even if you realize immediately that they don't know you very well. You would probably be stuck with them as your best three choices if you needed the letters within the next few weeks.

Some of the dimensions on which you might be evaluated include:

Ability to work independently
Ability to work with others
Academic performance
Commitment to the field
Communication skills (oral and written)
Industriousness
Intellectual ability
Integrity
Judgment
Leadership abilities
Maturity
Motivation
Organizational skills
Originality
Potential for teaching
Social skills

Do your referees know you well enough to evaluate you on the dimensions listed on the previous page? Ask yourself what you have done in the past to demonstrate to them that you rate highly on these attributes. This might identify areas where you have yet to make a positive impression, and allow you to plot a strategy for doing so. Just as importantly, this exercise might bring to your attention some damaging things about your behavior of which you were previously unaware.

How does knowing the dimensions on which you will be evaluated really help you? After all, you don't get to write your own letters of recommendation. But the truth is that even though you do not have direct control over them, you can still play a significant role in determining the quality of your letters.

If you have some idea of the dimensions on which your referees will be evaluating you, then you can take steps to ensure that when the time comes they will rate you highly. You may have few opportunities or little time to enhance the positive regard that one of your referees has for you, but if you are reading this with enough time before you will actually be requesting letters of recommendation, then there is much you can do. Some of these suggestions are discussed below.

One thing is critical to obtaining effective letters of recommendation: Students must put themselves in a position to be evaluated. This may mean taking directed-studies courses, volunteering to help a professor with research, or even just talking with professors outside of class. These types of activities should be ongoing in the years or months leading up to the application. And the student must perform well. It is clear, therefore, that acquiring effective letters of recommendation will take some planning far in advance of when you will actually be needing them.

What kinds of things will your prospective graduate supervisors be looking for in your letters? One thing that they may try to determine is how compatible you are likely to be with each other, in an interpersonal sense. They may be looking for some indication that the referees like and respect you.

What do you think an honest referee would say about your social skills or your ability to work with others if they saw that you have difficulty getting along with one of your fellow employees or with the other research assistants in the laboratory? It makes little difference who is at fault in such situations. It might be a simple clash of personalities. But that will not matter. You will only make yourself look good if you rise above the situation and handle interpersonal difficulties with dignity and maturity. In this situation, it would serve you well to let the other person create a bad impression of themselves but to avoid doing so yourself at all costs.

Who should you ask for a letter of recommendation?   Your choice of referees for your letters of recommendation will influence the effectiveness of those letters in at least two ways: First, your referees should be able to demonstrate that they know you well enough and in a capacity that would enable them to evaluate you on the relevant dimensions. Remember, your referees will indicate in their letters or on the evaluation forms the capacity in which they have known you.

A professor who you had for only one junior-level course may be expected to have little insight into your true potential. A professor for a senior-level course who gave you a very good grade for substantial written work, or for oral presentations, should be a better judge. If you are in an Honors program with a thesis requirement, your thesis supervisor or the director of the Honors program should be in the best position to evaluate you on the most important dimensions. (Review the sections of chapter 3 that describe some of the ways that undergraduate and graduate school are different).

A mistake many students make is to assume that they need letters from someone who will testify to their good academic performance. But your transcripts and standardized test scores already serve that purpose. Your letters of recommendation should go beyond your academic performance and evaluate you on other dimensions — dimensions that are even more relevant to success in graduate school than your ability to study textbooks and do well on exams. Some of these were discussed in chapter 3.

Another factor that can influence the effectiveness of a letter of recommendation is the *credibility of the referee*. This relates to several different factors. First, your referees will probably be asked to indicate how long they have known you. If they have only known you for a few months, some readers will assume that they don't know you very well.

The referee's credibility is also related to how much academic experience he or she has; that is, how long this person has been around, and therefore, how much experience he or she has assessing the potential of aspiring graduate students. A referee's academic experience can be estimated by considering his or her title or rank, as it is indicated on the evaluation form or below the signature line in the letter of recommendation.

Few undergraduate students have a clear understanding of academic ranks and because of this they fail to consider this important factor when choosing who to ask for recommendations. At most universities, the most junior, and still-untenured, full-time faculty members hold the rank of *assistant professor*. A promotion in rank to *associate professor* may accompany the attainment of tenure. Promotion to *full professor* is usually made on the basis of additional merit considerations. Many students are also unaware that some university instructors are not professors at all. Some schools hire part-time faculty members to teach undergraduate courses on a temporary contract basis. They may or may not be given a rank of assistant or *adjunct* professor.

In general, therefore, the more seasoned academics hold ranks higher than assistant professor. All else being equal, the professor with more years of experience will generally be viewed as a more credible referee. More senior faculty members may also have more experience writing letters of recommendation, and therefore, they may do a better job of it, although there is no guarantee of this.

If you are applying to a graduate program with a strong research orientation, the most credible referee will be someone who is also an active researcher in the same field. The more renowned this person is, the more credibility will be given to the endorsement.

The academic rank of a referee, while important, is still secondary to what that person has to say about you. Accordingly, the professor who knows you best will usually be your most important referee, even if that person is a junior faculty member or even a part-time instructor. One exception to this is if you are applying to a research-oriented graduate program — university and college teachers who are not active researchers might not be the best referees for evaluating your research potential.

There are good letter writers and bad letter writers   When I interviewed Graduate Program Directors and other admissions committee members for this book, one of the concerns that came up time after time had to do with the poor quality of many letters of recommendation. The complaints were not about the calibre of the applicants — they were about the lousy job that some referees do of writing letters!

There are good letter writers and there are bad letter writers. I am not referring here to people who write good or bad things about a student. The fact is that some professors simply do not know how to write an effective letter of recommendation, even when they have only the most glowing regard for the student. Ineffective letters are usually short, one or two paragraphs, and describe the student's qualities in vague or general terms. Good letters should provide informative anecdotes or some other revealing evidence to back up the positive general claims that they make about the student.

There is more that determines the effectiveness of letters of recommendation than how many good things the referees say about the student, or how well they back up their claims. It also matters how relevant the accolades are to the concerns of the potential graduate supervisor or admissions committee. The evaluation forms provided by some graduate programs request that referees comment on specific qualities of the students. For example, they might be especially interested in the students' writing skills, their commitment to a career in a particular field, and their industriousness, to mention only a few.

Referees do a disservice to their students when they write letters that fail to address the qualities specified in the instructions. Admissions committee members and prospective supervisors will not know why this has occurred. Is it because the referee simply did not read the instructions? Is it because he or she doesn't know anything about these aspects of the student? Or is it because these are dimensions on which the student is weak, and therefore, the referee decided to leave them out of the letter?

The lesson here is that someone with high regard for a student can still write an ineffective letter of recommendation, one that does little to enhance the quality of the student's application. So what can you do to ensure that your referees write positive and effective letters for you? Since you don't write the letters yourself, there are obviously limits to how much control you have over what goes into them. But there are some things you can do to make it more likely that your letters will be replete with favorable and relevant statements about you.

How to help them write effective letters   One reason why letters sometimes end up consisting mostly of vague compliments without any convincing demonstrations of the applicant's real merits is that the referee has to come up with everything from scratch. Professors are busy people, and it takes time and effort to compile truthful, relevant, and positive statements about a student, along with anecdotes or other evidence to support the claims. It can take even more time to compse it so it is truly convincing.

Ease the burden on your referees by furnishing them with material they can use to prepare your letter. Provide them with as much relevant information about yourself as possible. This would include a copy of your transcripts, a draft of a general self-sketch (discussed below), and a *c.v.*, if you have one (see chapter 9). Having the foresight to provide these materials might also add to your referee's impression of your good judgment and consideration.

Keep in mind that your referees will probably be busy writing letters of recommendation for other students around the same time as yours. The easier you make their task of writing your letter, the more likely they are to spend the time and effort needed to make it a good one.

One idea you might consider is to compile your own self-sketch, providing a brief synopsis of your qualifications, emphasizing some of the things that you would prefer to have emphasized in your letters of recommendation. You can write it in the form of a news release, just one or two short paragraphs. In many respects, it will be like a letter of recommendation that you've written for yourself! Or you can write it in point form if you prefer. Many professors like to see a year-by-year chronological summary of the relevant experience and accomplishments.

Give a copy of this profile to your referees when you solicit letters from them along with a copy of your transcripts and your *c.v.*, if you have one. Explain that the purpose of the profile is to help make their task of writing your letter easier, something that they can use as a quick reference.

Another benefit is that if more than one of your referees use this synopsis when writing your letter, there will probably be more consistency among them in terms of what they say about you. This consistency will strengthen the combined impact of your letters, and even more so if your personal statement is also consistent with the letters of recommendation.

If you decide to include a summary profile of yourself, be careful that your intentions are not misinterpreted. You are not taking over the job of writing your own letters. You are not asking the referees to simply endorse what you say about yourself. Nor are you implying that you want them to simply repeat the contents of your self-sketch in their letters. This is one reason why a self-sketch written in point form might be better than one written in prose form. On the other hand, you may be able to better control the emphasis you place on certain points if you write in prose form.

Ask your referees to emphasize in their letters any extenuating circumstances that account for a poor grade. Examples include such things as the course being a particularly difficult one that is outside of your major, or a course for which you had not taken a prerequisite course. Other reasonable justifications for poor performance in a particular semester include a prolonged period of illness, or the death of someone close to you. Explanations like these have a great deal of credibility in a referee's letter.

If you are applying to a program where you will have a graduate supervisor, and if any of your referees work in the same field as your prospective supervisor, then make sure you tell them who this person is. One or more of your referees may know your prospective supervisor personally, or at least know about the kind of research this person does. This may enable them to customize your letter in a way that makes it more relevant to the prospective supervisor's needs and interests.

Solicit your letters of recommendation a few weeks in advance of when you will be needing them. Students often underestimate the amount of time that goes into writing an effective letter of recommendation. I will spend as much as four or five hours writing a letter for a student whom I know well and have a lot of things to say about. Other referees may spend significantly more or less time, but I would suggest that if someone takes only ten or twenty minutes to write a letter of recommendation for you, then it is not likely to be much of a letter; it might say only good things about you, but it probably has little impact.

Requesting letters of recommendation a few weeks in advance is no guarantee that your referees won't still leave the task of writing them until the last minute and end up rushing anyway. It may, however, increase the likelihood that they will spend more time on your letters.

All of your efforts to help a referee write an effective letter can still fail to make a difference if the referee simply does not care or is an incompetent letter writer. There may even be a way to avoid this misfortune. Most of the people that you will solicit letters from will have previously written letters of recommendation for other students, either to support graduate school applications or scholarship applications. They might have a reputation concerning the kinds of letters they write for students. There may be other students around who know something about the kinds of letters that these individuals tend to write. One of the best sources of this information can be graduate students who have previously had to solicit letters of recommendation for scholarship or fellowship applications. In general, people with "successful" graduate students are good letter writers.

Proper ways to solicit a letter of recommendation   The task of approaching a professor to ask for a letter of recommendation can be stressful for many students. There is really no reason why it should be. Although it is true that you are asking them to take valuable time out of their busy schedules to do you a favor, with no obvious reward for them, it is also something they expect to be doing each year around the time that students are applying to graduate school. As long as you go about soliciting letters in an appropriate fashion, most professors will be willing to help you out.

> *A colleague told me about a student in one of his classes who came up with a wonderfully simple and sensible approach to setting up a good letter of recommendation. The student introduced herself at the beginning of the semester, told him of her career plans, and then informed him that she would be asking for a letter of recommendation at the end of the course. By distinguishing herself from her classmates early in the semester (i.e., making herself noticed) the student ensured that the professor would assess her relevant aptitudes and abilities whenever she showed them in some way, and by the end of the semester, he knew the student well enough to easily write her an effective letter.*

Remember that your interpersonal and social skills may be commented on in the letter, and the impressions that you make when soliciting the letter may contribute to the referee's attitudes about you. As we have already discussed, proper timing is important and it can be perceived as rude or inconsiderate when a request for a letter of recommendation comes too close to the deadline by which it is needed.

Your request can be made either in person or over the phone, but consider making it in two stages: First, you simply want to state your need for a letter of recommendation and ask whether they would be willing to write one to support your graduate school application. You are seeking nothing more than a verbal commitment at this point, but you should be prepared to answer certain questions. For instance, someone may wish to know why you are asking him or her and not someone else, what your graduate school or career plans are, how many programs you will be applying to, and therefore, how many letters you will need.

After they have agreed to write a letter of recommendation

for you, the second step is to arrange a brief meeting to give them any materials that will make their task of writing your letter easier. You may appear presumptuous if you come to their office to make your initial request carrying a copy of your transcripts or *c.v.* before they have even agreed to do this for you. This material should, therefore, be provided on a separate occasion, and usually at the same time that you give them any evaluation forms to fill out and the addresses and deadlines of the programs to which you are applying.

If you are applying to multiple programs and will be requesting more than one letter from your referees, then it is very important that you organize all of the material for them. Prepare a cover letter that lists the programs that you are applying to and the application deadlines (cover letters are discussed in chapter 9). If possible, put all of the information on one page. Make sure that you fill out as many parts of the evaluation forms as you can before giving them to your referees. It can be irritating to have to fill in line items on a form that the student could have and should have filled in themselves.

Some programs request that referees mail their letters directly to the department or to the School or Faculty of Graduate Studies. Other programs ask instead that letters are given to the applicants in a sealed envelope, which the referee signs across the flap, so that the applicant can submit the letters together with the rest of their application materials. If the application package that you receive does not include special envelopes for the referees to put their letters in, then provide envelopes with the proper mailing address already on them. Do not put your own return address on the envelope; if the letter is undeliverable for any reason, it should be returned to your referee, not to you. Make sure you clearly indicate to your referees whether they are supposed to send their letters directly to the program, or keep them for you to pick-up.

Remember to include the proper postage. It is amazing how many students forget to do this. Your referees have agreed to commit a great deal of their time and effort to doing you a favor. They have not agreed to pick up part of the cost of your graduate school applications.

Don't forget to express your gratitude for the time and effort that these individuals are going to spend trying to help you. Remember, a good referee who really wishes to help you will probably spend a few hours writing an effective letter of recommendation.

Your professors are probably busier people than they appear to be. You will owe them a great debt for this favor, whether or not their letters end up helping you get into graduate school.

> *If someone tells you that they would not write a good letter for you, do not be overly concerned until you get another qualified opinion. Although it may be the case that the first person does not have a good opinion of you, that does not mean that other professors share their opinion. It is impossible for someone to be right all of the time when it comes to assessing students' abilities or potentials.*

Student behavior and professors' attitudes   Professors notice more about students' behavior than most students assume. Some of the things that professors' observe shape their attitudes about a student's personal qualities. Students who might someday need letters of recommendation from professors must understand that their behavior today, whether positive or negative, may still be reflected in the attitude that a professor has about them one or two years from now. Naturally, most professors will come to like or dislike some students more than others. Nobody is going to write a good letter of recommendation for someone they dislike, so students should be thinking about how their behavior could affect their chances of having support from professors later on.

Some of the student behaviors that professors dislike are obvious: The worst include talking with classmates or rolling eyes or smirking while the professor is speaking, or frequently arriving late for class or leaving early without any apparent good reason. These actions indicate a total lack of respect for the professor and his or her work. Some students fail to realize that they are insulting a professor when they complain about the way an exam, paper, or project was graded. Students who are perceived as arrogant or pretentious, or as loud, childish, silly or immature, will find it difficult to reverse those attitudes even if they begin to behave more appropriately.

Some students engage in certain behaviors that they think will make a good impression on their professors, but with the opposite result. For instance, some professors encourage students to ask questions and voice their opinions in lectures, but dislike it when a student does too much of this and ends up monopolizing class discussions. Most professors don't mind if a student occasionally drops by the office to talk about academic matters, but some students do this far too frequently, or even worse, they take up their professors' time with their personal problems. Many of these same students see their professors in the hallway and expect them to stop to talk, failing to consider that professors may be busy even when they are in the halls — usually because they are trying to get to somewhere they need to be!

Among the behaviors commonly disliked are some that students would not expect professors to even notice or care about. One example is when students put in little effort and, as a result, do poorly on a midterm exam and later expect extra help outside of class to help them prepare for the final exam. Some professors may feel negatively about students who seem to be always anxious about minor things, or always stern-faced and much too serious, or chronically depressed. Everyone appreciates a compliment, but some students frequently compliment their professors in a manner that is perceived as manipulative.

Teaching assistants, most of whom are graduate students, also observe undergraduate student behavior and they may pass on their own stories to professors. Some professors have more disdain for certain negative behaviors than others, but everyone has some limit to what they can tolerate before they begin to dislike a student.

Most professors are reasonable and will overlook a few irritating behaviors if the student is otherwise very good. Most realize that students occasionally encounter personal problems or circumstances that legitimately take precedence over their studies. Even the most dedicated students may understandably become preoccupied for several days following a serious fight with a spouse. Although most professors are sympathetic enough to occasionally grant an extension on an assignment, or to reschedule an exam for a student with personal problems, repeated requests for this kind of special consideration may indicate that the student is unable to cope with adult life and responsibilities. Such a student is not likely to be able to cope with the demands of graduate school.

Students who will later be needing positive letters of recommendation must do more than avoid behaviors that professors dislike.

They should also give their professors some reason to have good opinions about them. It is not enough to "blend into the woodwork," as this will not give the professor anything positive to say in a letter.

So what are examples of admired student behavior that contribute to professors' attitudes of students they like? As with disliked behaviors or characteristics, some of the admired ones are obvious: students who seldom or never miss a class, are attentive and ask insightful questions, and who occasionally participate in class discussions. These give the impression that the student is interested in the course, and most professors will take them as compliments.

Among the student behaviors that professors like are some that students would not expect professors to even notice or care about. For instance, professors like to see students help each other. Sharing your notes with a student who missed a class might save the professor from having to spend extra time going over the material with that student. Professors like students who smile and say "hello" when they pass by outside of class. Some professors respect students who have the courage to disagree with them in class from time-to-time, as long as it is done in a respectful manner.

For the most part, the relations that exist between a student's behavior and a professor's attitudes about the student are nothing more than common sense. The important point to be taken from all of this is that you are being observed by your professors, and they are forming opinions about your character. Those opinions will be reflected in any letter of recommendation they might someday write for you. This is another reason why it is so important to start thinking about your letters of recommendation now!

> *The amount of time a referee spends writing your letter may depend primarily on how much time they want to spend doing you a favor.*

Additional comments on letters of recommendation   At some schools, letters of recommendation are confidential. That is, although the letters might stay in a student's file for years after acceptance into the program, the student never gets to see them. At other institutions, the letters are not confidential unless the applicant waives the right to see them. At a small number of schools, there is no confidentiality whatsoever concerning letters of recommendation; the applicant always has the right to see them. State or provincial laws often determine a university's policy on confidentiality of letters of recommendation.

It probably comes as no surprise that I recommend that you waive your right to see your letters of recommendation if you are given the opportunity to do so. There are at least two reasons why: First, the referees will know whether you will be able to see what they say about you. There is usually a place on the forms where you indicate whether or not you want to waive this right, and you indicate your choice before you give the forms to your referees. You might think that they would be more predisposed toward saying nice things about you if they knew that you might someday see their evaluations. Instead, you might actually offend them by not waiving your right to see what they say. This can affect the quality of the evaluations they give you. It might get you vague and unimpressive evaluations — ones that dilute the general quality of your application.

Another reason why you should waive your right to see your letters is because if you don't, then the prospective supervisor or members of the admissions committee might devalue the positive comments made in them. This could happen if they thought that your referees' comments were influenced by knowing that you might someday see what they said about you.

Summary   For most graduate and professional degree programs you will need three letters of recommendations from individuals who are qualified to judge that you possess skills, aptitudes, and character traits well-suited to graduate school. Your current professors will be your most appropriate referees, in most instances.

Some of the people deciding the fate of your application may be more interested in your letters of recommendation than any other component. Your prospective supervisors will want some indication that accepting you as their graduate student will be of some benefit to them. They may be interested in knowing what kind of person you are, and whether you are someone they would like.

One of the keys to acquiring good letters of recommendation

is understanding the need to get an early start on this task, ideally at least a year or more before you will actually need the letters. Students must put themselves in situations where they can be evaluated. This may mean taking directed-studies courses, volunteering to help professors with their research, or talking with professors outside of class.

Don't panic if your are already in your senior year and you realize that none of your professors know anything about you. There are still several steps you can take and mistakes you can avoid.

One of the factors that can influence the effectiveness of a letter is the credibility of the referee, which depends on how long they have known you, their academic rank, and the extent of their academic or research experience.

There are good letter writers and bad letter writers. You can help your referees write positive and effective letters by providing them with as much relevant information about yourself as possible, including a copy of your transcripts and a c.v., if you have one. You should also consider providing a brief synopsis of your qualifications, or a chronological summary of your relevant experiences and accomplishments. Be prepared to discuss your educational and career goals with them.

Solicit your letters of recommendation a few weeks in advance of when you will be needing them. Your professors may be very busy with other things, and they will probably be writing letters for several other students around the same time as yours.

Make your request in two stages: First, contact potential referees by phone, email, or in-person, and inquire about their willingness to write a letter of recommendation for you. Next, arrange a brief meeting to give them any materials that you have to assist them in writing the letter.

Carefully organize the forms and other information for your referees before giving it all to them. Be sure to provide the required postage, and don't forget to express your gratitude for their time and effort.

Remember that your professors probably notice more about your behavior than you think. Their attitudes and opinions about you will be determined by what they observe. Students must give their professors reasons to have good opinions of them and refrain from the types of behavior that professors dislike.

The Personal Statement

The personal statement (sometimes called the *statement of purpose, letter of intent, career goal statement,* or *biographical essay*) is perhaps the most difficult component to prepare for a graduate or professional school application. Like your letters of recommendation, the personal statement provides a nonobjective basis for evaluating whether you have the qualities needed for success in a particular graduate program. Its main purposes are to introduce yourself and to present those qualities that make you an excellent candidate for graduate school in general, and for the program you are applying to in particular.

Admissions committees and prospective supervisors look closely at personal statements with an eye to discovering things about you that are not available elsewhere in your application. It is their opportunity to see how you think, and how well you express yourself. It is their opportunity to learn who you are through *your* eyes. Accordingly, your personal statement reflects your personality and intellect. It is the component of the application where you show whether you have maturity, good judgment, and a professional demeanor. If ever there was a time for you to be articulate, it is now. If you are applying to a professional school in medicine, business, or law, or to a highly competitive graduate program in another field, there might be interviews later, but for most graduate programs you should think of your personal statement as a substitute for a brief personal interview with the admissions committee and/or prospective supervisor.

The most common mistake that students make is to fail to treat this part of their application with appropriate seriousness. It requires a great deal of thought and planning to write a good personal statement. You should expect to spend several days or maybe even weeks preparing several drafts before coming up with a good final product. If you spend only a few hours preparing and writing it, then it is almost certain to be a poor one. And none of the other components of your application will obscure or compensate for a poor personal statement.

There are two general formats for the personal statement, each of which differs in prevalence depending on the discipline. The most common format is the somewhat open-ended biographical essay in which you are free to explain whatever you think the admissions committee should know about you. An alternative format adopted by some programs is to have the applicant write a short essay in response to one or more specific questions, such as "Explain why you want a career as a _____." Some applications may include multiple essay questions, perhaps as many as four or five; this format is especially common for Business schools. Keep in mind that even programs offering the same degree can have vastly different requirements when it comes to the personal statement or essay.

> *Regardless of the format, you should treat the personal statement as a sales job — one where you are both the salesperson and the merchandise being marketed. As the salesperson, you should think of your personal statement from the point of view of the potential "buyer" — the prospective supervisor or members of an admissions committee. This way of thinking will help you understand why your personal statement can play such a crucial role in determining the overall impression that your application makes.*

It is critically important that you read the instructions carefully. Your response must show that you fully understand what is being asked of you. This is not always as easy as it sounds, as some applications can give rather vague instructions. One of the common mistakes that students make is to try to *guess* what the admissions committee is looking for with respect to the contents of a personal statement. There is no particular response that they are looking for, and it is always obvious when a student is trying to guess what they are expected to say. This will diminish your personal statement and can end up spoiling your entire application.

You should appear to have a long-term orientation with respect to your career plans and you need to indicate how graduate school fits logically in those plans. A surprising number of graduate school applicants have not yet defined in their own minds who they are and why they want to pursue a particular career. Be specific in defining your reasons. Do not say, for example, that you want a Ph.D. in Chemistry because you think you would make a good scientist. You want to present a *logical* rationale for wanting a particular career. This will require that you can explain your future objectives in light of your past. Accordingly, much of the content of your personal statement will be a recounting of select and relevant aspects of your past.

You will probably be applying to several programs, and it is important that each personal statement you send reflects that you have done your homework and understand what the program has to offer. Although there will be a great deal of overlap in terms of the content of the statements you send to different programs, the point here is that you must not simply send the same statement to each program. Your opening paragraph should be specially catered to each program.

Most personal statements in response to a question like "Why do you want to be a _____?" end up being similar and generally homogeneous. And also very boring! One thing you must try to do, no matter what kind of question you are asked, is to capture and maintain the reader's interest from beginning to end. This can be a formidable task, but if you are one of the few applicants who will compose a unique and interesting personal statement, you will have succeeded in satisfying one of your main objectives in the application process — you will have made yourself a *memorable* candidate, whereas most of the rest will have made themselves sadly forgettable.

> *The last thing you want to do is what most applicants do — most of them write a boring personal statement. Another big turn off is overly gushy or pedantic essays.*

Try to tell a story   So how do you create a personal statement that stands out above the rest of the crowd? Your statement should read like a story. You should be able to cite specific past experiences that made you interested in a particular career. Do not be afraid to include information that is of a very personal nature. After all, it is a *personal* statement. Make it clear how your application to this particular program fits in as the next logical step in your story.

You might have to think long and hard to find an interesting angle from which to tell your personal story. If there is something special in your past, then use that and build the rest of your story around it. Perhaps there were tremendous hardships you had to overcome to get to where you are today. Were you a misguided youth who found guidance and a sense of purpose in the wisdom of an older friend? Perhaps your father or mother have always inspired you to follow in their career paths.

Most of us think that our own lives have lacked drama. If you are like the majority of people in this respect, consider asking friends or family, or better yet, your academic mentor, to help you come up with something interesting about your past that you can use as the foundation for your story. This might be an important person in your life or an experience that has shaped who you are and played a significant role in bringing you to the point you are at today.

One of the most difficult things you are likely to face when preparing your personal statement is simply getting started. Remember, it takes time to be creative...so be patient. Ideas will come eventually. In fact, you should probably spend a while, perhaps several days, just thinking about a few things before you even begin trying to write. Try to answer the following questions about yourself, and keep notes of the responses you come up with.

What is special or unique about your personal history?

Are there any features of your life that would help the admissions committee understand who you are and where you are coming from?

Did you have to overcome any special hardships or obstacles to get to where you are today?

How and when did you first become interested in this field?

What has happened since then to make you even more interested in the field?

What are your goals with respect to a career in this field?

Do you possess any notable skills or abilities (such as leadership, analytical, computer, writing, public speaking, etc.)? How did you acquire them? What evidence could you point to that you do in fact possess these skills or abilities?

Do you possess any notable character traits (such as integrity, sensitivity, creativity, industriousness, persistence, etc.)? What evidence could you point to that you do in fact possess these traits?

In the opening paragraph, say why you are applying to this particular program. Perhaps your real reason is as simple as wanting to pursue a career in your field. But you don't want to just say so as simply as that. You should tell a very brief story that explains *why* you want that career. Do not merely imply that you enjoy your field of study. An intrinsic interest in your particular field of study is important, but it is important only to you. It is important to the admissions committee and to your prospective supervisor that you have enough extrinsic motivation to succeed in graduate school. Your stated intention to pursue a relevant career is evidence that you do.

It is not uncommon for students to graduate from college with no real knowledge of what is involved in the profession they are pursuing. Often, they have many misconceptions that can easily come across in a personal statement or interview. You must convey the impression that you have realistic ideas and expectations — that you really know what is involved in a career as, for example, a civil engineer, or an educational psychologist, or whatever it is you claim to want to become. Get advice. If you discover that you do not know much about careers in your field, consider it a blessing that you noticed this shortcoming now and not later on when it would be too late to correct.

Make sure that you elude to your relevant work experience somewhere in your statement. If you are reading this while you are in your senior year and do not yet have such experience, plan to get some during the next few months and you can refer briefly to those plans in your statement. For example, a Biology student might mention that he or she will be doing volunteer work at the local conservatory during the summer. A student of History might soon be volunteering at a local museum. Obviously, you must be honest in what you say you plan to do.

Here is a small hint about how to phrase your statement of these plans to obtain relevant experience: Make it clear that you are 100% certain to be actually getting the future experience to which you refer. Do not say that you *hope to* or *plan to* volunteer for relevant work during the summer. Instead, say that you *will be* doing this relevant work during the summer. Affirmative statements like this can induce someone reading your statement to attribute this experience to you in advance, which may obscure the fact that you do not already have the experience. It will also make you sound confident and in control.

Additional considerations for the personal statement   The quality of your personal statement hinges on *what* you say and *how* you say those things. Accordingly, the keys to a winning personal statement are selectivity of content, originality, and clarity of expression.

Selectivity means that you not only include the right information, but also that you exclude any inappropriate information. I have noticed that most students say basically the same kinds of things in their personal statements and most of what they say does not belong there. Do not waste time and space describing the classes you have taken and the kinds of grades you have achieved, unless it is to highlight the fact that you have taken certain courses that make you especially well-suited to the academic demands of the graduate program. Another situation where you might want to discuss specific courses and grades is if you need to explain why a grade or GPA does not reflect your true abilties. Most students probably should not waste space in their personal statement discussing their grades. Everything about your course selection and grades is available in your transcripts, and the people reading your personal statement can look at your transcripts if they want to know the details.

Referring to academic achievements or other accomplishments prior to college is, in most cases, a mistake. To mention the fact that you obtained an A+ in every high school class while you were also captain of the basketball and football teams would create the impression (probably accurate) that you do not know the difference between relevant and irrelevant background. Participation in varsity sports as an undergraduate will seldom be of any significance. And incidentally, few graduate programs care about *legacy* status — having a close relative who attended the college or university in question.

Avoid controversial subjects. You don't know who will be evaluating your statement or what attitudes they have. You do not want to risk offending anyone. Avoid politics and anything that would reveal your own political biases. The same goes for religious views; they normally do not belong in a personal statement. Do not say anything or raise any issues that could be considered by someone to be bizarre.

Avoid jocularity. This is not the time to try to be cute. You will only offend the members of the admissions committee. They will think that you are not serious about getting into their program and may be insulted.

> *You need to put a great deal of thought into what you say in your personal statement, and just as importantly, what you leave out of it. Your choices of what to include will tell the reader something about your judgment.*

Originality means that you avoid saying the same old tired things that everyone else says in their boring and unmemorable personal statements. You want to write a statement that grabs the readers' attention at the very outset and holds their interest through to the end. Think about this: For many of its readers, your personal statement provides a first impression of you. Do you want their first impression to be that you are ordinary and dull and lacking originality? Of course, by "original," I do not mean peculiar or bizarre.

Clarity of expression means that what you write must be logical. It must be written with proper syntax and grammar, and free of spelling mistakes and typos. This is not just because a spelling mistake will make the reader think you cannot spell. A statement that contains these kinds of errors will make you appear unprofessional and careless. The reader might wonder upon seeing these kinds of mistakes whether this is a reflection of the kind of written work you would submit in a graduate course.

Have one or two friends read your personal statement and ask them to give you frank feedback and advice. If possible, ask this same favor of one of your professors, one who knows you well and whom you feel comfortable asking for the extra favor. Ideally, this should be a professor who is also serving as a referee for one of your letters of recommendation. This way the professor can keep in mind the content of your personal statement when preparing his or her letter and strive for consistency in terms of the kind of person that he or she describes and the one described in your statement. Refer to the advice given in the previous section on how to request a letter of recommendation and use the same measure of politeness and tact when asking one of your professors to read and provide feedback on your personal statement.

Whether you are required to respond to specific questions about yourself and your plans, or to write a general personal statement, keep the statement reasonably brief. Most programs put a page or line limit on the personal statement. Even if they do not specify exact limits, it is essential that you don't ramble on about insignificant aspects of yourself or your history. This can only make a bad impression. Remember, your letter will be read by busy people — people who have many others to read and who will get annoyed if they have to spend more time than they want to reading any individual statement. A few short paragraphs covering one-and-a-half to two pages is almost always enough, unless the instructions in your application package specifies that you need to provide particular details that require more space than this.

If you are applying to graduate school in a research field, then you need to make a convincing case that you are interested in this field, and specifically in the area in which your prospective supervisor does research. Even if it is a program in which you would be assigned to a specific supervisor only after some time in the program, or if you will receive periodic supervision by multiple faculty members on a rotational basis, it should be apparent from your statement where you are expecting to fit in eventually. Put in something specific about the person or place you are applying to.

Do not write a letter that begins with something like, "I have been reading Dr. so-and-so's famous papers with great interest."

You should be more tactful and reserved. You should actually read some of this person's papers, and refer to them in a way that demonstrates that you really know about his or her work. I have received letters from students claiming that they were interested in my research. I could not tell whether they had actually read any of my published papers and understood what my research was about, or had merely read the titles.

You must give the impression that you have researched the program to which you are applying and the faculty who reside in that department. It is not uncommon for applicants to say that they are interested in a specific topic or research area within their field, and then ask to have a particular faculty member as their supervisor even though that individual's research is entirely unrelated. These students really blow it by demonstrating how unprepared and uninformed they are. It is worth repeating here that your statement should include something specific about the person or place that you are applying to.

If you are applying to law school or medical school, there might be more to say in your personal statement. But do not try to say everything. Highlight two or three or maybe four important points and keep it at that. The people on the admissions committee will appreciate reading a concise and well-organized personal statement rather than a long, boring, and irrelevant one.

Remember, your goal is to write a personal statement that will leave the reader with a positive and memorable impression of you. Therefore, you want to refer to your strengths and any notable qualities you possess that should help you succeed in graduate school...and especially in this specific program. Put this information in the second paragraph, but be very careful here. Do not go overboard in talking yourself up. Keep in mind that many professors (myself included) get very turned off by students who have delusions of grandeur. Self-confidence is a good thing — in fact, it is one of the qualities I look for in a graduate student — but students with inflated ideas about how good or important they are often alienate the people whose support they need.

Your situation might include specific problems that can be addressed in a personal statement. Perhaps there have been extenuating circumstances that explain why your GPA is lower than it should be? Were you *seriously* ill for any extended period of time (i.e., over at least one entire semester)? Did you have to deal with the break-up of your marriage and a battle for custody of your children?

Perhaps you took courses from outside your major or specialization that are known for their difficulty. For example, while I was a psychology major, I took organic chemistry and molecular genetics courses. These courses were very demanding to most students, especially those without a background in chemistry or genetics. They required most of my study time, and this hurt my grades in other courses I was taking at the same time. When I pointed this out to my prospective supervisor, it raised his opinion of my grades. Perhaps it also drew his attention to the "easy" course selections of one or more of the applicants with whom I was competing!

You should consider providing a personal statement even if it is not explicitly required in the application, although you are unlikely to encounter such a situation. The worst thing that can happen is that it will be discarded and not be considered with the rest of your application. But there is also a chance that it will not be discarded and will remain a part of your file. The potential impact of a personal statement can be amplified in cases where it's not required, just because your file will be one of the few that include one. Some people may be impressed by the fact that you included in your application an informative story about yourself and your reasons for applying to graduate school. It shows that you know what you want and that you are very serious about their program.

Just remember that your statement will be read by people who are trying to form an impression of who you are and what you are like. The impression will be good only if the statement is good; a bad statement will make a bad impression. If a statement is not explicitly required in the application, then it would be a worse mistake to include a bad statement than to include none at all.

There is an added benefit to putting all this work into writing your personal statement. By the time you are done, you will definitely know how to respond to the questions of who you are, what you are looking for in a career, how you intend to get there, and how you got to this point in the first place. As you will see in the next section and in Chapter 8, this is excellent preparation for a preselection interview with an admissions committee, or for a face-to-face meeting or telephone interview with a prospective graduate supervisor.

> *Members of admissions committees are annoyed when they have to spend more time than they want to reading any individual statement. So they probably won't. Make sure yours is read in its entirety by making it interesting and reasonably brief.*

Summary   Some graduate or professional school applications require you to answer specific questions in a personal statement or an essay. Many students make the mistake of underestimating the importance of this part of the application. You should expect to spend several days or weeks on it in order to do a really good job.

Some programs request that the statement be made within a defined space on the application form. Make sure you understand exactly what information is being requested. Read the instructions carefully and respond to every question. You don't want to give the impression that you cannot read and follow instructions.

Do the necessary research prior to writing your personal statement (review chapter 4 for ideas on how to learn about careers in your field and choosing the right graduate program). You must give the impression that you have researched the program and the faculty who work in the department.

Try to make your statement or essay read like a story. One of your goals should be to grab the reader's attention at the outset and hold it right through to the end. One of the hallmarks of an effective personal statement is originality. If there was a specific event or experience that got you interested in a career in your field, then tell this story.

Your first paragraph needs a great deal of attention. In fact, you might spend most of your time getting this paragraph just right. It is crucial that you do so because it sets the tone for the rest of the story. Once you have worked out the first paragraph, the rest will be easier.

Be specific in explaining yourself and your goals. Do not say the same old boring and totally unoriginal things that admissions committees see all the time — things like, "I want to be a psychologist so that I can help people".

Be selective. You may not have room to say everything that seems worth saying, so make every sentence and phrase count.

Describe your relevant qualifications. Here, it is important to demonstrate good judgment. Do not waste ink on something that makes no impression, or perhaps even a bad impression by being irrelevant. Be sure to refer to your relevant work experience.

Show a draft of your personal statement to a friend, or to a professor whom you know well, and ask for feedback. You will probably need to write several drafts before you have a really good personal statement.

Preselection Interviews

Many graduate programs conduct preselection interviews as part of their admissions process, although most do not. The prevalence of such interviews varies considerably across fields, and across different programs within fields. They are most common in professional degree programs, such as those in law, business, or medicine, and in the most competitive graduate programs in other fields.

Preselection interviews are conducted strictly by invitation. In programs that conduct them, this is usually the final step in their selection process. Only those who survive to make it onto a short list of the the most promising applicants will be invited for an interview. The interview is an applicant's final make-it-or-break-it opportunity.

You will find out whether a program you are applying to conducts preselection interviews when you receive the application package. If you notice that interviews are conducted for the top-ranked applicants, you should take several steps to prepare in advance so that if you are invited for an interview you don't blow your chances of being accepted into the program after getting this close.

Find out when the interviews are usually conducted so that you can schedule your activities during this period accordingly. Do your best to arrange your life so that you have no other major commitments during the potential interview period. Keep in mind that you might have to miss a few classes to attend an interview. Inform your professors in advance that it may become necessary for you to reschedule any exams or term papers that have due dates during that period. Almost any professor would cooperate with such a request, and most would appreciate receiving the request far in advance.

You should do whatever you can to attend an interview if you are invited for one. In fact, these interviews are considered *necessary* for acceptance into some programs. Make sure that you prepare in advance to have the financial means in place to make the trip. Some programs provide financial assistance to aid interviewees with travel costs, but this is rare, and it would be unwise to expect such assistance. It would also be unwise to decline an invitation to an interview because of the cost involved. Such a decision on your part would be a clear signal that your priorities do not include getting accepted into this program.

If you are unable to pay for your own trip, say so. They might make an exception and offer to help you out in some way. But make it clear that you would be willing to hitchhike to get there if you had to because you are so seriously interested in them.

Even though you have already impressed the admissions committee on paper — otherwise you would not have made their interview list — you must remember that more applicants will be invited for interviews than there are available slots in the program for new students. To put this another way, some of the applicants who are invited for an interview will end up being rejected, and those who do attend have a distinct advantage over those who are invited but do not attend.

It is always possible that something unavoidable will come up and you won't be able to attend the interview. Telephone interviews might be possible, so you should ask for one if it is absolutely impossible for you to attend an interview in person. You must make it clear that you sincerely regret not being able to come to the interview, and that your inability to do so does not reflect a lack of interest in their program. You must not come across as aloof, disinterested, or pretentious.

Remember, the key to success in applying to graduate school is to do things that will set you apart from the other applicants.

The real purpose of preselection interviews   You might wonder why some programs go to the trouble and expense of conducting face-to-face interviews when the rest of the application materials provide so much information about an applicant. The answer is in a notion that was discussed earlier: Most graduate programs are interested in recruiting the best *people* they can find from among their applicants, and this selection may require more than just a consideration of academic and related credentials.

The primary purpose of most interviews is not simply so the admissions committee can obtain more information about the applicant's background. Although the interviewers may be trying to fill in certain informational gaps that remain following their assessment of the application materials, their main interests will be in evaluating what the applicant is like as a person. They may also be looking for evidence to confirm the positive impressions that were made by the application materials. In many respects, the functions of the interview are similar to those of the personal statement, so you might wish to review the previous section.

It helps to keep in mind the interviewers' objectives. They will be judging whether you would be a pleasure to have in their department. They may be trying to determine how well you would fit in with the other graduate students and faculty. These impressions will have already emerged partially from your letters of recommendation and your personal statement. At this point the interviewers may be looking for inconsistencies or other warning signals.

Interviews also provide a means of assessing applicants' verbal communication skills, their ability to listen and to think quickly and flexibly, their self-confidence, assertiveness, how they respond to stressful situations, their general level of maturity, and even their appearance.

A secondary purpose of most preselection interviews is to get more information on some of the applicants' credentials that were mentioned in their applications. For example, an applicant's personal statement might have eluded to extensive analytical or computer skills without providing enough information for the admissions committee to fairly assess those skills. The applicant may be asked to elaborate on these things. Applicants who mention that they are fluent writers and speakers of a second language may be expected to show evidence of this in an interview.

How to prepare for an interview   There are two common types of preselection interviews: a series of one-on-one interviews with members of the admissions committee and perhaps other faculty members, and interviews in which a single applicant meets to answer (and ask) questions of a group of faculty members or an admissions committee. A third but far less common format is to have all of the interviewees meet at once with the entire admissions committee. You have to prepare the same way for all three types of interview.

The first thing to do is review everything you know about the program, the rest of the department and its faculty members, and the campus. This should involve any notes you took during your advance research about the program and its faculty, anything that you were sent, or that you have learned through correspondence with someone in the program. You might plan to make another visit to the library to review what information you can find in any program guides, brochures, or calendars. If you have access to the Internet, visit the program's web site. Don't be content with reviewing what you already know — try to find out even more.

You should also review everything that the *program* already knows about *you*. Carefully review the personal statement, essay, or essays that you sent with your application. List the specific claims you made about your background, experience, and goals. You need to make sure that you do not contradict anything you said previously in your statement or essays. This will not be a concern if you have been, and continue to be, completely honest and forthcoming when discussing your personal history and credentials.

The next step is to prepare for the kinds of questions that you are likely to be asked. Some of them are likely to be tough, and no matter how good you are on your feet, you will do better in the interview if you can prepare and practice your answers in advance. Of course, you cannot anticipate the exact questions you will be asked, but you can approximate what some of them will be, and a good response might include portions of your prepared answers. Prepare and rehearse answers to the following tough questions:

How did you hear about our program? Why do you think it is the right program for you?   The interviewers want to know that you are genuinely interested in their program, so you must show them that you are. Display sincere interest by indicating that you were attracted by specific strengths or orientations of the program, that you know they have good people in the program, and that they provide high-calibre training.

Tell me about yourself.   Write out and rehearse a two-minute summary of who you are, what skills you possess, and what you have done that is outstanding. Many students are too modest in an interview. They have a compelling personal statement and *c.v.*, but when they get to the interview they say "Shucks, I'm not special." Obviously, you do not want to brag or exaggerate your credentials. But the interviewers do want to hear what you think are your strong points.

What are your career goals?   The trick to answering this question is to sound sincere in your desire and definite in your plans. If your plans are too vague, that may be seen as indicating that you lack the focus needed to get through graduate school. Your career goals should provide justification for your application to this particular program. That is, try to describe a career that would require the kind of training that you would receive in this program. However, be careful not to describe your career expectations too narrowly, as this can make you come across as presumptuous and naive, or outside the prospective supervisor's focus.

What are your weaknesses?   Do not say that you have trouble getting up in the morning, or that you have difficulty finishing things. Say something that will make you look good. For example, "I tend to speak before I think," or "I tend to focus on detail and initially miss the broader perspective." Most students have these problems; being aware of them is positive. Say how you are trying to improve.

What are your strong points?   Focus, commitment, drive, willingness to work hard, or any other good qualities that make you likely to succeed. Don't list too many. A good number is two or three, but you need to be able to elaborate on them a bit.

Why do you think you are the right candidate for our program? Where do you think you will fit in best?   Regardless of how they ask this question, your response should emphasize the same things. Do your homework in advance and make sure that you know enough about the program to discuss specific aspects of it, and to avoid describing expectations that would not be met by this particular program.

How to handle the interview once you are there   As the interviewee, this is another opportunity for you to sell yourself. But, this *does not* mean that you should take a "used-car salesman" approach. Although you will be asked questions about your interests, goals, skills, and experience, you need to understand that it is mostly your personality that is being assessed. **It is essential that you be yourself in an interview. Be completely honest and sincere in how you answer every question.** Your goal is not to come across as being perfect. Social psychologists have shown that people with a few flaws or imperfections are judged as more likable than people that appear flawless or "perfect." Of course, no one is really perfect, but some people are able to do a good job of concealing their imperfections from others, and they mistakenly believe that this is going to make others appreciate them more. The best tactic is really no tactic at all. Just act naturally.

Preselection interviews are understandably stressful for almost any applicant. There is a great deal on the line, and how well candidates perform in the interview will have much to do with how well they are able to deal with the stress. Beyond stress management, there are also a number of basic things that one should try to do or try not to do in an interview. A marvellous book, *Sweaty Palms: The Neglected Art of Being Interviewed*, by H.A. Medley, is in most college and university libraries and in many bookstores. It is a popular guide to successful interviewing, and I recommend it highly if you have time to do some additional reading. Complete reference information can be found in the *Resources* section (Personal Statement, Essay, and Interview Guides).

Remember that first impressions can have a lasting impact on how one is regarded by others. Applicants who make a positive first impression at an interview are most likely to be accepted into the program. Those who make negative first impressions have a major hurdle to overcome, and they may never really recover from it.

Whether or not you instil a positive feeling in the interviewer will partly depend on many small things that occur during an interview, some of which will be consciously noted by the interviewer and some of which will influence them at a more subtle, unconscious level. All of these little things will contribute to the overall impression you make, so you must be mindful of each of them and do not treat any of them as trivial or inconsequential.

One of these small things is punctuality. You must show up in the right place at the right time. In fact, it is a good idea to plan to arrive about fifteen minutes before the scheduled time. This will not only indicate your eagerness and reliability, but planning to arrive early will give you some protection against unanticipated problems, such as a traffic jam, or trouble finding the right building or room. Make sure that you are absolutely certain of where you have to be and exactly when you have to be there to begin the interview.

The rest of your itinerary should be taken care of for you, and the responsibility of having you in the right place at the right time will be partly taken out of your hands at some point. But the responsibility will be entirely yours at the beginning. The interview can't start without you! This seems so obvious that you might not think it is worth mentioning here. But some people get so excited at the invitation for a preselection interview that they neglect to get the information they need about the time and location, or else they forget to record it in a place where they can find it when they need it.

Medley's book lists several other small things that interviewees should be mindful of, most of which are matters of common courtesy. One of them is to remember the interviewer's name. Do not use this person's first name unless you are invited to do so. Such an invitation would be unlikely at this stage, although once you became a graduate student you might be invited to do so.

Another one of Medley's tips is: do not offer to shake hands unless the interviewer offers a hand first. If you are shaking hands with someone, offer a good firm grip. Weak or limp hand shakes turn some people right off. Obviously, you do not want to grasp the other person's hand with so much force that you hurt them. Smile and say, "Pleased to meet you, Dr. _____." Do not sit down until the interviewer asks you to do so or offers you a chair.

At this point, the interview is ready to begin. Try to relax a bit and avoid being distracted by interesting things in the room that might be begging for your attention. You need to relax, but you don't want to act too laid back. You are expected to be a bit nervous, and the interviewer might think there is something wrong with you if you aren't.

Focus on the interviewer. Make eye contact while listening and while speaking. This should provide immediate feedback on how the interview is going. Moreover, it can be disconcerting to interviewers when one avoids eye contact. Listen closely so that you understand exactly what is being asked.

Your responses should be honest, sincere, and on topic. As already mentioned, you must not contradict things that you said previously in your personal statement or essays with respect to your interests, your qualifications, or other aspects of your background.

For interviews that have the format of several successive one-on-one meetings with members of the admissions committee or other faculty members, you also need to be consistent in what you say to each individual interviewer. You will likely find yourself answering certain questions more than once. And you should expect that the interviewers will be comparing their notes afterwards. Again, the easiest way to avoid crossing yourself up is to be as honest as possible when answering all questions.

What might be more difficult, but equally important, is to present yourself in a way that is consistent with how your character was conveyed in your personal statement. If your statement was a good one — and it probably was if you were invited for an interview — then it likely displayed some passion for the field of study. The same sense of passion should be apparent in how you respond to your interviewers' questions. Your statement probably implied that you are certain about your career goals and that you have sound reasons for applying to this particular graduate program. The same sense of focus should come across in the interview.

Do not criticize others, and be prepared for traps that are aimed at trying to get you to expose whether you possess this nasty quality. If you are asked why you obtained a mediocre or poor grade in one of your important courses, do not place the blame on the professor or on the undergraduate curriculum. If the interviewer mentions that one of the referees for your letters of recommendation expressed a minor concern with one of your qualities, do not become defensive or imply that the referee is mean or stupid. Admit that you may possess the shortcoming in question and indicate that, having become aware of it, you are are now prepared to eliminate it.

Remember to ask questions   You will have some control over the content of the conversation, which you should try to exercise once in a while. If you merely sit there and give flaccid responses to all of the interviewer's questions and comments, then you may come across as timid and boring. All interviewees will answer questions, so if this is all that you do, you will not be setting yourself apart from the other applicants with whom you are competing.

Do not make the fatal mistake of spending the whole interview answering questions and not asking any yourself! It is vital that you find opportunities to ask questions about the program, for at least three reasons:

First, asking questions about the program will make it clear that you are genuinely interested in it. But you have to choose questions carefully so that the interviewers are not left with the impression that you haven't learned anything from your own research of the program.

Before the interview, make a list of unanswered questions about the program that you still have. These should all be things that you do not already know about. You may end up with a list of one or two dozen questions, but do not expect to ask all or even most of them. Many will be answered for you before you even get an opportunity to ask them. Try not to leave all your questions for the very end of the interview. Work some good questions into the conversation.

Make sure that the questions on your list are things that you really do want to know about. Think about each of these questions and eliminate from your list any that might be construed of as especially naive or off-base. As a general rule, the most appropriate questions are those about how certain aspects of the program will directly affect you while you are a student there. For example, you might ask how students in the program should expect to allocate time among the various activities of study, research, training, and other responsibilities.

The second reason why you must ask questions is to demonstrate that you have the conversational skills and confidence to do so. Your referees may have commented on your oral communication skills. You have to live up to their positive claims.

The third reason why you must ask questions is to actually find out the answers! If you have important questions about the program, then you will need answers before you can make your decision of where to go if you happen to be accepted into more than one program.

Do not take total control of the conversation with your questions. Know your place as the interviewee, and let the interviewer take primary control of the situation. You will need to be on your toes and make sure you occasionally slip a good question into the conversation. When you do, make sure that it is on topic, and that it is clear why you are asking. This is easily accomplished if you have listed and studied your questions beforehand, as recommended above. Rehearse your questions in advance.

If by chance you are not directly asked to describe your relevant experience in work related to your field, then find a way to work it into the conversation. Do not assume that the interviewer has read your personal statement recently and doesn't need to hear about its contents again. In fact, the best way to highlight important information is through some acceptable amount of repetition. If people read in your personal statement about a research project you helped with, and see a reference to this experience in one or more of your letters of recommendation, and are reminded once more during an interview, they are not likely to forget to consider this important information when making a decision on your application.

All of this advice on how to act during an interview makes a great deal of sense right now, while you are reading it. But what are the chances of you remembering it all during the interview? Probably not that great if all you do is try to commit this chapter to memory. You will do better if you can get some practice with a little role-playing. Ask a friend to play the role of interviewer. If you are on very good terms with one of your professors you might ask for a mock interview to help you prepare. This could be very helpful in identifying those aspects of your performance that need attention.

If you are unable to recruit someone to help you prepare for your interview, try going through imaginary interviews by yourself. Picture yourself actually sitting in a stranger's office and answering the types of questions you can anticipate. Watch and listen to yourself closely with your mind's eyes and ears. Imagine yourself remembering all of the advice that you have read about. This type of imagery really works, and just like with overt role-playing, the greatest benefits come with practice. Another advantage of covert role-playing is that you can do it on the airplane on your way to the interview.

Your appearance   Appearances say a great deal about a person. One of the main messages that will be taken from your appearance in a preselection interview is your regard for the seriousness of the proceedings. You want to appear clean and well-groomed. You should dress up enough to show that you have respect for your interviewers. For an interview at a professional school, it would be appropriate to dress in a suit and tie or other formal, businesslike attire. Less formal attire is appropriate for preselection interviews in most other fields. The most important thing is to appear like a mature and responsible adult.

This is not the time to dress unconventionally. Note here that I am not advising you to misrepresent who you really are. Nose rings and tattoos are okay with most university professors, so long as it is clear from your grooming and attire that you are treating the interview seriously. Don't forget to smile. No one wants to invite a sourpuss into their workplace.

Summary   The main purpose of preselection interviews is for the graduate program faculty to get to know what you are like as a person. You should do whatever you can to attend such an interview if you are invited.

Prepare by reviewing everything you know about the department and the program, and everything they already know about you. Present yourself in a way that is consistent with how you were portrayed in your personal statement, essays, or cover letters.

Compose and rehearse answers to the types of questions that you are likely to be asked, as well as some of your own questions. Study your questions before the interview and try to memorize the most important ones. You don't want to be trying to think of questions on the spot, even though some appropriate ones may come to mind during the interview.

Pay close attention to what the interviewer is saying at all times. If you are not sure how to interpret a question, ask for clarification before you attempt to answer it.

Remember the little things that affect the general impression you make, such as punctuality, good manners, a positive attitude, neat appearance, and a smile.

Try to relax a bit so that you aren't fiddling with your hands or fumbling when you speak. It might help to remind yourself that you have already made a good impression or else you would not have gotten to this stage. You want to be confident, but not cocky.

You are more likely to feel comfortable and to remember all of the foregoing advice if you rehearse the interview *process*, and not just your prepared answers to the types of questions you expect to be asked. This is best done via a mock interview with a friend, or else by imagery and mental rehearsal.

III. Going Beyond the Requirements

The information and advice in the previous chapters should enable you to be among the few graduate school or professional school applicants who will maximize the impact of each component of their application. Equipped with this new understanding and insight, you are already far ahead of most of your competition for admission into the programs that are best for you. You should not stop there, however, because there is still much more you can do to improve your chances of getting in.

So far we have dealt only with those admissions requirements that are published by programs, and the specific components of an application that most programs require applicants to submit. However, there are additional considerations, many of them extremely important, that are not outlined in the application packages sent out to students. Understanding what these factors are and how they can influence the selection decisions will allow you to take steps that will greatly improve your chances of being accepted.

Most of the ideas and strategies outlined in the next three chapters will not even occur to most students. Even those helpful professors who coach students through the application process are unlikely to explain or even consider some of these things. The applicants who will have the most success are those who understand the significance of these factors and who incorporate the advice into their application planning.

From the outset, you will be treated differently as a graduate student. You will be expected to think and behave like the scholar, scientist, artist or professional that you are training to become. If you dread public speaking and wish you were better at it, graduate school will provide you with the experience you need.

Chapter 8

Major Steps That
Most Students Miss

Contacting Prospective Graduate Supervisors

The advice in this section is aimed at students who are applying to a program in which a faculty member will serve as their graduate supervisor. **One of the most important steps you can take is to make personal contact with your prospective supervisor prior to applying.** I find it peculiar that most students fail to do this. As a result, they are still strangers when the time comes for the faculty member to consider their application.

In this section, we will discuss several advantages of making direct contact with your prospective supervisors. By the time we are done, this preapplication contact will seem absolutely essential. In fact, I believe it is so important to establish correspondence with prospective supervisors prior to applying to their program that the topic of this section was the main reason why I originally decided to write this book!

Many students think that it is inappropriate to contact a prospective supervisor or a Graduate Program Director prior to the application period. They reason that it may be perceived as manipulative, and thereby make a bad impression. But in fact, the opposite is true. As long as the contact is made for legitimate reasons, like those discussed below, then establishing some preapplication correspondence can be one of the most important things you do to enhance your prospects of being accepted into a program.

> *Timing is important when you are contacting a prospective supervisor or a Graduate Program Director. So long as your attempt to make contact comes before the application, then it will likely be seen as a very sensible move on your part. If it comes after you have sent your application and before the selections have been made, it is more likely to be seen as manipulative.*

Some of my colleagues have told me that they would never agree to supervise a student who failed to contact them before applying. Some told me that no matter how good students appear on paper, if they do not possess the good sense to contact them before applying, this indicates that they lack awareness and good judgment, in general. Even if you are applying to programs where you will not have a specific supervisor, you should still know who the faculty members are with interests that match yours and consider directly contacting them.

Surprisingly, contact from potential students is not universally popular among faculty members. Some find these contacts to be a nuisance, and they prefer instead to first screen applicants' credentials and then contact only those who meet or exceed their specific criteria. However, there are at least three good reasons to ignore the fact there are some faculty members who would not be influenced by preapplication contact: First, this is such a minority group that there is a good chance that none of your prospective supervisors belong to it. Second, even if one of them did, you would not know. Third, I have never heard anyone suggest that preapplication contact actually hurt anyone's chances of being accepted.

It is important that you make contact with prospective supervisors in an appropriate way. A phone call can be much more useful than a letter, for reasons that will be discussed later. Still, it is usually best to initially contact a prospective supervisor by regular mail or electronic mail, then follow up a few weeks later with a phone call or more email. Students often complain about being unable to reach faculty members, or that they never return their calls. Email should facilitate this process.

Why it is so important to make preapplication contact   The correspondence you have with a prospective supervisor has important benefits for both of you. Some of the benefits to you are outlined below. You should realize why this contact is so important for the prospective supervisors, too. They know that they will have to give a new graduate student a good deal of attention over the next few years. In order to convince them that they want you as their student, you need to know what it is that they want in a student.

There are certain qualities that anyone would want their graduate students to possess. But some people's criteria also include other "special" qualities, which may play the biggest role in determining how an applicant measures up. Many professors want to ascertain whether they will *like* prospective students before they make the commitment to supervise their graduate work. This type of priority might seem surprising at first, but it makes perfect sense when one considers that the student/supervisor relationship usually lasts for a few years, and no one wants to spend a few years working with someone they don't like.

With so much at stake for graduate faculty members in selecting the right person to supervise, why would any of them take the risk of accepting a complete stranger, someone with whom they have never spoken, when there may be other applicants with whom they have had some personal contact? Some faculty members will take this risk from time to time, but quite often they end up regretting that they paid too much attention to the student's credentials and too little consideration to the student's personality and other important characteristics. Other graduate supervisors, having made this mistake once or twice, have vowed never to make it again!

The opportunity to develop your own impression of the prospective supervisor is equally important to you. You need to remember that the faculty members in any graduate program are all different individuals. A graduate student/supervisor relationship with each one of them would be different. You want to spend the next few years working with someone you like. On the other hand, you probably do not want to work with someone just because you like them and you think that the two of you would be good friends.

Be on guard for signs of potential exploitation. You do not want to become someone's lab *employee*, working as their graduate student merely because you fill a specific role in a research "production line." This happens more often than you might think. In many cases the supervisor is not even aware that this is an inappropriate way to supervise graduate students. But you should also remember that the relationship you have with your supervisor does not exist to benefit only you. A trade-off of sorts is to be expected. You help them to conduct their research, or whatever scholarly, literary, or artistic work is involved in the discipline, and in the process of doing so, they help you to develop your own skills and expertise.

Remember, you want to make your name the one that is special to your prospective supervisor. Most other students who apply to work with the same individual will simply send the required application materials to the program. They will not personally contact the prospective supervisors or do anything else to make themselves stand out. They will be relying only on how they look on paper. You will be far ahead of the competition by giving your prospective supervisor a reason to remember you, before they even get to see your application file. This often happens automatically when you pick up the phone and call, because it is so rare for applicants to have the good judgment to do so.

> *Some graduate program faculty members never actively recruit graduate students. Instead, they wait for applicants to come along and sell themselves.*

How and when to make contact   The best way to contact your prospective supervisors is with an in-person visit. There are many advantages for both you and them in having a face-to-face meeting before anyone makes a commitment. But, even if you plan to meet them in-person, this will first require an initial contact from a distance in order to make arrangements for such a meeting.

By telephone.   One problem with phone calls is that you never know in advance whether you are calling at a time that is convenient for the other person. He or she may be busy with any one of a number of things, and unable or uninterested in talking with you at the moment. When the person answers the phone, be ready to quickly say who you are and why you are calling, and then immediately ask whether you are calling at a convenient time. Whether or not you are asked to call back later, the important thing will be that you were polite and thoughtful enough to appreciate that a person might not be able to talk to you at that particular time.

A better approach that also reflects thoughtfulness and consideration is to send a letter or an email message introducing yourself and indicating that you will be calling in a few days, or else asking when it would be a good time to call. When you do eventually call, make sure first that you are prepared to answer the following questions: *What do you know about them? How do you know about their work? Why do you think it is a good idea for you to have them supervise your graduate work? Where do you think you will fit in best? How do you think they are going to benefit from having you as their student? What are your short-term education or research plans? What are your long-term career goals? Have you applied for any scholarships or fellowships? What other programs have you applied to?* You might not be asked any of these questions, or any other question for that matter. But then again, you might be. And if you are, your replies had better be good ones because they will have a large part in determining the first impression you make.

By electronic or regular mail.   Send a brief cover letter to prospective supervisors stating that you will be applying to their programs and that you are interested in the possibility of having them supervise your graduate work. Try to say in just one or two sentences why you think there is a good match.

In most cases, it is inappropriate to send a copy of all of your application materials directly to your prospective supervisor. There are a few things, however, that it might be appropriate to send. One example is a copy of your transcripts. This can help the prospective supervisor get an overview of your background. It is not necessary to go to the expense of sending an official copy of your transcripts. A photocopy will do. The official copy or copies will still be included in the application package.

You should not send a copy of your personal statement or any letters of recommendation. These items will be in your application package and the prospective supervisor will get a chance to look at them later. Attach a copy of your *c.v.*, if you have one, and a copy of any published papers or abstracts from conference presentations on which you are an author. Make sure that you explain briefly in your cover letter if the subject of these publications does not reflect your current interests or the kind of research you would expect to be doing if you were accepted into the program.

At this point in time, your main objective is simply to let them know that your application will be forthcoming, that you hope they will look over your enclosures, and that you will call or email them in a few days to discuss matters further.

At some point, you really should make a phone call. There are limits to what you can ascertain about a person's character and demeanor through written communication. Speaking to each other will provide both you and the prospective supervisor with an opportunity to circumvent these limitations and get a better idea of what the other person is like.

Your first contact with a prospective supervisor should be a few weeks or more before you will be sending your application. If you contact them months before they see your application, then you should try to make one or two more contacts during the intervening period so that they remember who you are.

You need to know whether they wish to or intend to take on a new graduate student this year, and this should be one of the first things you ask. It happens often that students apply to work with a particular faculty member with whom they seem to be a perfect match, only to find out later that person was not planning to take a new graduate student that year. Many professors will take on a new graduate student only once every few years, whereas others are more active in graduate supervision and might tend to take one or two new students in most years. Some may cease to be active researchers and stop taking graduate students altogether. The norms vary widely across disciplines.

The point is that you are wasting your time, effort, and money if you do not find out early whether the prospective supervisor is actually interested in taking a new student. Of course, none of this applies to some master's programs where students are assigned to supervisors only sometime after they are accepted into the program.

If you think that your application might be screened out by the admissions committee because of weak grades or poor scores on a standardized test, then you must alert your prospective supervisor to this possibility. Otherwise, they might never see your application file! But if you alert the prospective supervisor that your application is coming and is at risk of early rejection for whatever reason, then they can usually tell the admissions committee that they still want to consider you as a possible graduate student and look over your file. This way your application stays in the competition.

This is where your prospective graduate supervisor often begins working to get you admitted. They may explain to the admissions committee that you have been in touch and that they know more about you than simply what your grades and standardized test scores look like. Or they may cite other reasons for wanting to take responsibility for supervising your graduate studies. Many students are accepted primarily on the basis of a faculty member stating that they want to supervise the student.

> *Do not underestimate the importance of this: If it happens that someone you want as your supervisor also wants you as a graduate student, this can sometimes be all it takes to get accepted into the relevant graduate program, provided that you meet other minimum requirements.*

Ask the right questions   As previously mentioned, when you call a prospective supervisor you should be prepared to talk about why you are calling, why you are interested in them as a mentor, what your grades are like, your background and experience, etc. It is just as important that you have your own questions to ask. In fact, one of the main things that you will do when you contact your prospective supervisor is ask questions.

It is important to ask questions for two reasons: First, that is how you will get the information you need or want. Second, when you ask the right questions, it demonstrates that you are bright enough to know what is relevant and assertive enough to seek out what you need to know.

Many questions will occur to you as you read and consider the advice in this book. Write them down and imagine yourself asking them. Have a list of questions ready before you make your call. If you simply try to remember them all, you may forget some of the most important ones.

Ask them about their current research, if applicable. This is something that you need to know about before you make your own decision about studying with them. You might wish to know how many graduate students they already have, and whether their current students collaborate on projects or work solely on their own.

Ask about financial support if this is a relevant issue. Are there sources of income available for graduate students in the department? Most departments at most universities offer some kind of opportunity for financial support to their graduate students. Typical appointments that pay a wage or salary include teaching assistantships, research assistantships, laboratory demonstrators, and course instructors. Some departments, faculties, and schools have awards for highly qualified graduate students. Consult the *Resources* (Funding Guides) and the section on financing graduate school in chapter 3.

Some researchers have grant money that they can use to support graduate students. But do not ask your prospective supervisors directly whether they have this kind of funding to support your studies. That would be too presumptuous. Let them bring it up themselves if they want to.

A potential supervisor should be able and willing to answer questions that are of importance to you. For example, he or she should be able to describe to you the process for reviewing applications to their program, and what kind of financial support is available for successful applicants. Most individuals do a good job of telling students what they need to know, including certain things that the students might not have considered. But do not be surprised if someone is uncertain about the answers to some of your questions.

If the prospective supervisor does not seem interested in speaking with you and answering your questions, you should ask yourself whether you really want to work with that individual. Good graduate supervisors take a genuine interest in the development of their students. They are willing to take the time to discover what they need to know about new applicants, and provide new applicants with the information they need to make an informed decision. If people seem disinterested in you when you are applying, they will likely also be disinterested in you later.

There are probably dozens of questions that you would like answered. Obviously, you would leave most people with a bad impression if you tried to ask twenty or thirty questions during a ten-minute phone call. But you don't have to actually ask that many questions in order to get that many answered, either. Most of the people you speak with will understand why you are asking these questions, and many of them will try to tell you other things that they think you should know, some of which will also be on your own list of questions.

Asking questions about relevant things will indicate that you are someone who takes affirmative action to address your sensible concerns. Either consciously or unconsciously, the other person will know that you possess good judgment. And good judgment is often the greatest asset that a graduate student can have.

There are certain questions that you might be tempted to ask, but should not. This would include mundane questions about aspects of the program requirements that you can get from other sources, such as the material sent to you in your application package, or from the Graduate Program Director or the program secretary.

Do not take it personally if someone decides not to accept you. It does not necessarily mean that you are unworthy of acceptance. There are many reasons why faculty members might not want to, or be able to, take new graduate students in any given year. They might lack the means of providing financial support for a student, or for the costs of a student's thesis research. Maybe they already have as many graduate students as they can manage right now. Perhaps they expect to be on sabbatical leave next year, or they plan to retire within the next few years. These are all valid reasons for rejecting you, even though none of them have anything to do with the quality of your application.

How much correspondence is too much?   There is no rule of thumb. Be persistent, but at the same time, be aware that there is often a fine line between being persistent and being a pest. Keep in mind that professors are busy people. Some students mistakenly believe that their applications are very important to prospective supervisors, and that these faculty members will, therefore, be keenly interested in frequent correspondence. Someday you may in fact come to be very important to them and to their work, but for now you are not. If you try to impose too much on their time, you will probably be snubbed. Do not call or email for inane reasons during the preselection period.

You won't need to make too many calls if your timing is appropriate. The problem is, you don't know what their schedules are like. Again, email gives you more leeway with this because the people receiving your messages can reply when it is convenient for them to do so. Still, you do not want to inundate them with email every other day, either. Even a brief reply to an email query takes time. If you attempt to have too much correspondence, you run the risk of irritating the other person. That is the last thing you want to do.

> *A word of caution: If you get a verbal commitment from someone who is willing to supervise your graduate studies, you must not suspend all of your efforts that you have directed at other schools, not even if this is the person with whom you most wish to work. Until you have a written acceptance from the department, anything might happen to cause a verbal agreement to fall through. You should always have options to fall back on in case the unexpected happens. Do not burn bridges that you might need to cross later on.*

Summary   If you are applying to programs where you will have a graduate supervisor, one of the most important steps you can take is to make personal contact with your prospective supervisors prior to applying. This contact should be made several weeks before the application period, and the best way to do it is either by regular mail or electronic mail, followed several days or a few weeks later with a phone call or more email.

By making this contact, you will be setting yourself apart from the majority of other applicants. Some prospective supervisors may be impressed that you had the good judgment to call them. Preapplication correspondence is an important part of your research into who your prospective supervisors are, what they do, and what they are like on a personal level. It is also the simplest way to determine whether a particular faculty member is even interested in supervising a new graduate student.

Preapplication correspondence with prospective graduate students can also be important for many faculty members. It is an opportunity for them to learn the details of your interests and background. They may wish to ascertain whether you are someone whom they would like as a person. Be prepared to talk about why you are interested in having them as an academic mentor, what your grades are like, your background and experience. Also be prepared to ask relevant questions of your own.

Keep in mind that there is often a fine line between being persistent and being a pest. Professors are busy people. Do not call or email for inane reasons.

Writing Effective Cover Letters

We are often reminded of the importance of first impressions in shaping peoples' opinions about us. Indeed, considerable attention was paid to this matter in chapter 7 when we discussed how to handle preselection interviews. If the first impressions that applicants make at an interview are positive, their chances of eventually being accepted into the program are greatly enhanced. If, on the other hand, this first impression is negative, then the task of reversing it becomes an uphill battle that will likely end in defeat.

Although an interview is often the first opportunity for members of the admissions committee or prospective supervisors to meet an applicant *in-person*, it is not really the first opportunity they have to form an impression of the applicant. Instead, the very first contact that an applicant has with those individuals who will ultimately decide the fate of their application is either through a written application form, or through some sort of cover letter that the applicants include with their application materials, or in the case of a prospective supervisor, through a cover letter as part of some preapplication correspondence that is initiated by the student.

Most graduate school applicants give relatively little thought to cover letters, perhaps in part because these letters have such a seemingly straightforward purpose — to introduce the student and explain his or her intentions of applying to the program. Some well-organized applicants spend dozens of hours researching potential graduate programs and supervisors and preparing other components of their application packages, but give only a few moments of consideration to a cover letter, the document that will serve as the basis for the very first impressions that they make. In light of the well-known importance of first impressions, this lack of concern for the cover letter is a major problem.

Cover letters can sometimes have considerable impact on the success or failure of a graduate school application. This is because the cover letter sets the tone for the rest of the application. A well-written letter can spark interest and enthusiasm for your application, whereas a poor letter can undermine an otherwise well-planned and executed application strategy. A cover letter enables the reader to discern your organizational and writing skills, your sense of good judgment and priorities, social skills, personal style, and your ability to focus on important matters and to avoid irrelevant ones.

Will admissions committee members really be trying to assess these things when they read your cover letter? Probably not. To be truthful, this is usually not the place where people focus their attention when considering candidates for their programs. That is, they seldom read cover letters with an eye to uncovering positive indications of an applicant's potential as a graduate student. On the other hand, they will not be able to avoid noticing any obvious *negative* signs that might present themselves in a poor cover letter. Your main objective in writing a good cover letter, therefore, is not so much to make a positive impression as it is to avoid making a negative one!

When do you need to include a cover letter?   There are at least three situations where a graduate school applicant may need a cover letter, either by itself, or to accompany other materials:

The first is when writing to graduate schools to request additional information on the programs they offer and/or to request their application packages. Even this letter is potentially important, as it may be retained by the program and later placed in your file with the rest of your application materials. Do not ask detailed questions in this initial letter because many of them will be answered with the materials they send you. This is, however, the right time to ask about financial aid from the department or university, because the application deadlines for such aid often come prior to the program application deadlines.

Another situation that calls for a cover letter is when a student wishes to contact a prospective supervisor prior to submitting an application, as was discussed in the previous section. Students should send a copy of their *c.v.* , if they have one, and a cover letter that introduces themselves and announces their interest in applying to the program. If students do not have a *c.v.* , then the cover letter may be all they send.

The third situation that may call for a cover letter is when submitting the application to graduate programs that do not require a separate application form. A cover letter is not usually needed to accompany an application form, but in some cases it may be a good idea to include one. This would include instances where important and relevant information about you is not covered in another part of the application, if test scores or a letter of recommendation are expected to arrive late, or if there was a lapse in your education that requires explanation.

A book entitled, *The Perfect Cover Letter*, by R.H. Beatty, is the best one I have found on the topic. The book deals primarily with cover letters for job applications, but most of the advice applies equally well to cover letters that students would write to a prospective supervisor or to accompany a graduate school or professional school application.

The purpose of a cover letter   The task of writing an effective cover letter requires that you first understand its two main purposes: to explain your intentions and to introduce you and the relevant aspects of your background to the admissions committee or prospective supervisor. Like the personal statement or biographical essay, a cover letter is a sales document in which you attempt to convince the readers that they will benefit from accepting you into their program.

Accordingly, graduate school applicants should write their cover letters from the perspective of the admissions committee, or that of the prospective graduate supervisor, depending on who the intended reader is. What are the readers' priorities? What specific needs are they seeking to satisfy? If you do not know the answers to these questions, it will be easy to write a cover letter that is dull and uninteresting and that emphasizes things about you that have nothing to do with the readers' needs. If, on the other hand, you follow the advice in chapter 4 and do a thorough job of researching the graduate schools you are applying to, and where applicable, the faculty members there who might serve as your graduate supervisor, then you will be well prepared to address the readers' needs in your cover letter.

The needs of the admissions committee are generally to find applicants who have good scholarly potential, as evidenced by past academic and related accomplishments, and who also have priorities and interests that fit with the program's objectives and specializations. If you are writing a general application cover letter for a program that you have researched well, you will be able to describe your interests and qualifications in a way that appeals to these needs of the admissions committee.

The needs of the prospective supervisor may have less to do with finding an applicant with scholarly promise than with finding one who shows good potential for fitting into a specific program of research, although most will be looking for both of these things. The applicant's research interests will generally have to be in line with the prospective supervisor's. The type of research or other work that the prospective supervisor does might necessitate that graduate students possess certain technical knowledge or skills (Recall the story in chapter 4 about the student who didn't have the requisite background or skills that she would have needed to participate in the research that was being conducted in a highly computerized laboratory). If you are writing a cover letter to a faculty member with whom you think you might like to do your graduate studies, then a genuine understanding of this person's research will enable you to present your qualifications and interests in a way that targets the needs they have for a specific kind of graduate student.

All of this should sound familiar to you. It is similar to the

advice given in chapter 7 on how to write an effective personal statement or essay. Of course, there are also important differences between
a personal statement and a cover letter. For one thing, brevity is even
more critical in a cover letter than it is in a personal statement. A cover
letter might be two or three short paragraphs, about one full page,
and not more than two pages at the most.

Cover letter format   A proper cover letter has at least the following
six components, although in some instances there may be more: The
minimal components are 1) the date, 2) the address of the recipient, 3)
the greeting or salutation, 4) the body of the letter, 5) a complimenta-
ry closing, and 6) your signature with your full name printed beneath
it. The *format* of a letter refers to its physical layout and design, including the order and position of each component within the letter, the
proper use of indentation, alignment, spacing within and between
components, and margins.

　　Rather than using a lot of space here to describe how to
properly format each of these six main parts of your cover letter, I
suggest instead that you dig up a few short business letters (we all
receive these kinds of letters in the mail from time to time) and take
a look at how they are formatted. You may notice a few variations
among them, but you will surely notice some consistencies as well.
Decide which one you think looks the best and copy the format. You
can also find standard forms for cover letters in word-processing
programs, as most of them have templates for many kinds of business documents.

　　If you wish to learn about proper cover letter format in more
detail, read R.H. Beatty's book, *The Perfect Cover Letter* . Complete reference information can be found in the *Resources* section (General
Advisement Guides). Check in your school's library for other books
on writing cover letters.

　　Use a conventional format for your cover letter. Doing so will
increase the letter's effectiveness by improving its general readability
and by conveying a positive impression of professionalism and good
judgment. A cover letter that fails to conform to an acceptable format
will send a negative message about you. Superficial matters such as
these can seem trivial and silly, but they are nonetheless important to
many people, and you can never know if one or more such people

will be reading your cover letter and forming an impression of you on the basis of what they see in that letter.

There are a few basic ideas to keep in mind with respect to the general appearance of your letter. If it is disorganized and messy looking, this will suggest that you and your work are similarly disorganized and messy. By contrast, a well-organized and neat looking letter will send the message that you are similarly organized and careful in your work. You cannot afford to make a bad impression by writing a cover letter that is poorly formatted, contains spelling or grammatical errors, or is otherwise sloppy looking.

Do you have to type your cover letter? Doesn't a neatly hand-written letter convey a kind of personal touch? Yes, it may, but this is not the place to be informal or personal. Instead, a serious and business-like demeanor is in order. If at all possible, your letter should be neatly typed using clean paper and a new ribbon (no smudges), or if you are using a computer, the letter should be printed on a high-quality laser printer. If you do not have access to either a good typewriter or a computer and laser printer, then pay the few dollars it costs to have someone else type or print your letter for you.

Remember how it was emphasized earlier that graduate school applicants should try to make themselves stand out from the crowd by doing some things differently than the way most applicants do them? This is a good place to remind you that doing things differently does not necessarily mean doing things in an unconventional manner. Do not make the mistake of assuming that an unconventional format will make your cover letter stand out from the crowd and impress the reader. The effect would probably be just the opposite. Remember, cover letters help to form first impressions, and you do not want to give the impression that you are antisocial, nonconforming, foolish, immature, or ignorant. Besides, in my experience, a good cover letter that conforms to conventional standards is such a rarity among graduate school applicants that writing a letter like this can go a long way to help set you apart from the majority of applicants.

A little less formality is required if your first written contact with a prospective supervisor is made through electronic mail, and for email it is entirely appropriate to exclude some of the components that would be part of a proper cover letter, such as the date and the address of the recipient. For the most part, though, you should do the wise thing and generally format your email message the same way you would a regular cover letter.

Content for an effective cover letter Exactly what kinds of things should be included in a cover letter? What should be left out? Not surprisingly, the answers to these two questions depend on whether it is a general application cover letter that will be used to introduce yourself and your intentions to an admissions committee, or a cover letter that is used to make contact with a prospective supervisor. Although there will be similarities between these two kinds of letters, there are also significant differences.

When the letter is intended for an admissions committee. Most cover letters written by graduate school applicants provide little or no information beyond that which is already available elsewhere in the application. Such letters, therefore, add no positive value to the application. This is not meant to imply, however, that your cover letter should *only* contain information that is unavailable elsewhere. In fact, it is a good idea to use this letter as a means of highlighting some of your most important credentials. This can save the reader from having to find all of the important things that might be buried throughout various parts of the application package, and it reduces the likelihood that the most important things about you will be overlooked.

The introductory paragraph should state your interest in applying to this graduate program. That sounds simple, but the real challenge is to state this intention in a way that grabs the reader's interest so that they want to read the rest of the letter. You must strive to get the reader's attention at the outset, because the rest of the letter will be of no use if it is not even read. Most cover letters are boring and they don't provide much useful information. If it appears from the first couple of sentences that your letter is like this, the rest of it might not be read.

One way to evoke interest with your introductory paragraph is by using specific knowledge about the program that you obtained in your advance research. For example, suppose you are a psychology student who wishes to pursue graduate training in an experimental field, specializing in cognitive development in children. You have discovered a doctoral program in a Psychology department where there are faculty members conducting research in cognitive development in preschool children and other faculty members who study cognitive decline in aged individuals. You might state in your cover letter that you are interested in this program because it clearly provides opportunities to learn about and conduct research into issues related to cognitive development throughout the normal life-span, and not just in young people. Such a statement would make it obvious that you have done a thorough job of researching this particular Psychology department.

Most admissions committee members will be impressed to find that an applicant has done his or her "homework" because the majority of applicants either will not have done so, or if they have, they will fail to make this fact evident in their cover letters. Noticing that you have taken the time to learn about their department and graduate program, most admissions committee members will return the favor by spending the time needed to carefully read your letter. Just be careful here not to flaunt the research you have done, or you may come across as insincere and manipulative.

Another way to get the attention of an admissions committee in your introductory paragraph is to make use of a personal contact that you have within the department. For instance, if you are applying to a program in which you will be doing graduate studies under the supervision of an individual faculty member, then you will most likely have someone specific in mind as a potential supervisor, and following the advice given earlier, you will have established some contact with this individual prior to submitting your application. Hopefully, he or she will have replied to your written or telephone contact, and by the time you are actually ready to submit your application the two of you will have had additional correspondence.

You should make it clear to the admissions committee that you have established this friendly relationship with a faculty member in their department. This is easy to do, but it must be done in a tactful manner. For example, you would not indicate this personal contact with such a direct and obviously manipulative statement such as, "I know Dr. Brown." Instead, you might state that you have been keenly interested in the program ever since you learned of one of its unique features during a conversation with Dr. Brown.

Just keep in mind here that your goal is simply to make the reader sufficiently interested that they will continue to read what you have to say. They will be interested in you if they know that one of their colleagues knows who you are. But be careful. You must take a subtle approach to using this strategy of eliciting interest in your cover letter. Even if you have multiple personal contacts within the department, it would be best, in most cases, to elude to only one of them. You do not want to sound like you are trying to impress by "dropping names."

The first few sentences of a cover letter set the tone for the rest of it. If there is nothing special about the opening sentences, the rest of the letter might not even be read.

Once you have the readers' attention, it is time to sell them on the idea that you have something of value to offer them. You have to do this quickly in just a few sentences. It is usually at this point that the task of cover letter writing suddenly becomes difficult. The problem is in deciding which things to highlight, and which to leave out. The important thing to remember is that you must write the letter from the perspective of the intended reader. It does no good to refer to those things that you are most proud of if they do not address the needs of the reader.

One or two sentences in either the first or the second paragraph should provide a background summary of your education and training experience that is most relevant to your graduate school application. This would include such things as relevant work experience, years of experience, any degrees held and/or the degree program you are currently enrolled in, and degree completion or expected completion dates. The summary should be very brief. Its purpose is simply to indicate that you have the necessary background, without going into detail. The details of your education and training will be dealt with in other parts of the application.

When the letter is intended for a prospective supervisor. The cover letter that one uses to make initial or subsequent contact with a prospective supervisor prior to or during the application process shares several characteristics with the general application cover letter, but it also has its own unique requirements. This should not be surprising to you, since you now appreciate that a good cover letter is written with the reader's needs in mind, and the needs of individual faculty members differ from those of a graduate program as a whole.

If you follow the advice in chapter 5, you will be applying to more than one graduate school, and therefore, will be preparing more than one cover letter. By now, you should know that it would be a bad idea to write a generic letter to send to all of the people on your list of prospective supervisors. There may be certain parts that are the same for each letter, but you will need to customize each one to reflect the fact that you are acquainted with each individual's work and that you have something substantial to offer as a graduate student. The potency of your cover letter will be directly related to the quality of your advance research into the work of the prospective supervisor.

The tactic of getting the reader's attention by mentioning a departmental contact will not apply in most cases when writing a cover letter to a prospective supervisor, because it is *they* who will usually end up being your departmental contact. The best way to spark a prospective supervisor's interest in your letter, and in you, is to display a good knowledge of who they are, what they have done, and what they do now.

Keep in mind that, unlike the admissions committee, the prospective supervisors have no obligation to read any of the material you send them. It is important to realize, therefore, that if a cover letter is poorly written, the prospective supervisor might not even bother to look at your curriculum vitae. If the letter is difficult to read or inappropriate from the start, then the prospective supervisor might be so turned off that they don't even read the whole letter. It's all about first impressions!

In general, you will put less emphasis on your past academic performance in a cover letter to a prospective supervisor than in a general application cover letter. Grades often have little relevance to the needs of graduate supervisors. They will be more interested in knowing whether you have demonstrated an aptitude for research or other scholarly work of a similar nature to their own. It is not that the admissions committee is uninterested in this, it is just that they will also be concerned with the likelihood that you will do well in graduate classes. The prospective supervisor will have more specific concerns with respect to research or other relevant work.

Determining the current focus of someone's research is not always as simple as it sounds. Naturally, the place to start is by looking up some of this person's most recent published work. The problem is that there can often be a lag of up to a few years between the time when original work is actually done and when it finally appears in the public domain. In the meantime, the person's work might have taken a significant turn in a new direction.

> *Remember, it can take some extra effort to ensure that you are up-to-date with someone's research. Do not assume that because someone was working on a particular problem three years ago that they are still doing the same thing now. If your information is out-of-date, your assumptions will be wrong about what this person is studying and what kinds of interests he or she is looking for in a graduate student. Many professors have their own World Wide Web pages. Any important information that you find there is likely to be reasonably current.*

Look for recent *trends* in people's work. Again, the letter must address the needs of the prospective supervisor, and these needs may change over time. If you are able to convey the fact that you understand where their research focus has been in the past and where it is now, it will be clear that you possess a keen interest in their work. Once again, the effectiveness of your letter in convincing the prospective supervisors to take a closer look at you as a graduate student candidate will depend on how much time and effort you have put into learning what you can about them and about their work.

The point here is simply to be mindful of the possibility that an individual's research might have undergone a recent change with significant implications for the apparent match with your own interests, and with your ability to adequately anticipate and address their needs in a cover letter. I don't believe that this would happen often. In fact, in the vast majority of cases, recent publications will be fairly representative of one's current research activities.

> *Avoid describing your interests too narrowly. A description that is too narrow could inadvertently remove you from further consideration if it does not fit into the supervisor's present and future research plans.*

An effective cover letter ends with some remark that compels the reader to take some kind of follow-up action, usually to look over any enclosed material or to reply to the applicant following some consideration. This part of the letter has somewhat less relevance in a general application cover letter than in a letter to a prospective supervisor. In the former case, all that you can wish the admissions committee members will do is look over your file and confer a recommendation regarding your application. They are going to do this anyway, whether you put the idea into their heads or not.

Your attempt to elicit interest from a prospective supervisor with a good cover letter will often be of little use unless there is further correspondence and an opportunity to learn more about each other. You might close an initial cover letter with a line like, "Please feel free to call me at (555) 555-5555 if you wish to discuss these matters." The onus is now on the prospective supervisors to reciprocate with some kind of communication if they think they might be interested in you.

If your letter and enclosures have convinced them to take a closer look at you, then they might give you a phone call or a brief written reply. If they don't, then your correspondence will come to a dead stop. You will have no idea whether they read your cover letter and your curriculum vitae, or whether they even received them. Perhaps they received your letter and became quite interested in learning more about you, but soon thereafter became distracted by something else and basically forgot about you.

You can avoid this possibility by taking responsibility for the next contact. You might end your letter with something like, "I will phone next week in order to determine whether you are interested in my candidacy." As you can see, the idea is to ensure that reciprocal correspondence is established. And since they know that you are going to phone next week, they are more likely to be prepared for that call by looking over your letter and any enclosed materials.

Additional considerations for cover letters   Good judgment, manners, and tact, are all hallmarks of an effective cover letter. Attention to details can make a big difference in how well these attributes come across. For example, you need to select a closing that is appropriate for the nature of your relationship with the reader. In the case of an initial contact with a prospective supervisor whom you have never met, or in a cover letter to the relatively anonymous members of the admissions committee, use a somewhat formal closing such as "Yours truly," "Sincerely," or "Sincerely yours." Closings such as "Regards," or "Best regards," are less formal and are appropriate for letters to someone with whom you already have a friendly relationship.

The proper greeting or salutation to use in a general application cover letter might be "Dear Members of the Admissions Committee," or something to that effect. If you are writing a cover letter to prospective supervisors, the salutation must include the title appropriate to their position. In many cases, you will be writing to someone who holds a Ph.D. or some other type of doctoral degree. The proper way to address them in a cover letter is with the title of "Dr.". Do not use "Mr.," or "Ms.," or "Mrs." The use of the proper title shows courtesy and respect for the person to whom you are writing.

Make sure that you spell their names properly! It goes without saying that this is important, but you would be surprised to find out how often mistakes are made. Some surnames have several common variations. For example, Johnson and Johnston, Douglas and Douglass, or McNeil, McNeill, MacNeil, etc.

Think about what it might suggest to prospective supervisors if you are unable to spell their names properly. The most obvious message is that you have not done your homework and that you know very little about them and their research. After all, how could you fail to encounter their name several times during the process of investigating their work? I once received a letter from a student who claimed to be interested in my research, yet he addressed the letter to "Dr. Dave Momby." This person's credibility was shot by the first few words of his very first contact with me. Perhaps he really did know that my name is "Mumby," and the error was just an innocent typo. But even if I knew this to be the case, it would tell me that this individual was careless, and therefore, not the kind of person I wanted to have as a graduate student.

The general style or tone of a cover letter can reflect a great deal about the personality and social skills of its writer. Negative impressions are formed when the writer comes across as being arrogant or conceited, or conversely, as being too timid or lacking confidence. Do not make self-deprecating statements or imply that you only *hope* that you can excel in graduate studies. Instead, you should convey the utmost confidence that you can and will outperform. Avoid sounding shy or apologetic, or implying that you have any doubts about your qualifications.

On the other hand, you do not want to brag about your past accomplishments or exaggerate your strengths. Be careful not to overuse superlatives. You should express a humble yet confident attitude about your strengths and accomplishments, without saying anything that would take away from them. Self-confidence is an essential attribute that most successful graduate students possess.

Avoid sounding too pushy or aggressive. For example, the statement in your letter that is intended to impel the reader to take follow-up action should be an invitation or a suggestion for such action, not an order. For example, "Please feel free to contact me at your convenience if you wish to discuss..." would have an appropriate tone, whereas "Please contact me when you get a chance so that we can discuss..." sounds more like an order than a suggestion. It sounds pushy.

Never be critical of others. Many students make the mistake of blaming their past shortcomings on circumstances beyond their own control, or even worse, on other people. Occasionally, for reasons that are mysterious to me, a student will think that they can strike a friendly accord or impress a faculty member by being critical of someone else's research or ideas, especially when they are at odds with those of the faculty member in question. Instead, it just indicates that these students lack respect for others and their opinions, and for the diversity of views and approaches characteristic of most academic and research areas.

Do not forget the importance of courtesy in making good first impressions! The final comment in any good cover letter (prior to the closing) should be an expression of gratitude to the readers for their time and consideration in reading your letter and whatever material was enclosed with it. This is simple to do and uses up little space. When this kind of common courtesy is missing from a cover letter its absence can stick out like a sore thumb, leaving a negative impression. A simple remark, such as "Thank you for your consideration," is all that is needed. If the letter is a response to an invitation to an interview, then something like, "I look forward to meeting you," is a courteous way to end the letter.

Summary   Good cover letters are characterized by:

1. Conventional cover letter format, decent overall appearance, proper grammar and spelling.

2. An introductory paragraph that grabs the reader's attention and compels them to read further.

3. Content that targets the needs of the reader.

4. A brief summary of educational and other training background.

5. A statement that moves the reader to take follow-up action to your letter.

6. Courtesy, including a statement of appreciation for the reader's time and consideration.

Bad cover letters are often characterized by an absence of one or more of these features, but additional elements can sometimes appear in a cover letter to make it ineffective or lend to it creating a damaging impression of you. For instance, poor cover letters often have a lack of focus and ramble on about things that are not relevant to the central issues. A cover letter must be brief and concise; there is no room for irrelevant statements or remarks.

If you are often heard criticizing others behind their backs, soon everyone will assume that you do the same to them, and most will come to distrust you.

Chapter 9

Little Steps Where Most Students Stumble

Proper Timing and Following Up

Admissions committees get irritated by having to consider incomplete application files. In fact, many programs strictly adhere to their deadlines and will not consider an application if any of the required components are missing or late. Even when you are applying to a program that allows a little bit of leeway, perhaps a few days or even a week or two past the published deadline, you should never miss that deadline. For one thing, you usually do not know in advance which programs have absolute deadlines and which ones allow a bit of flexibility. Even when they allow you to get away with it, being late makes a bad impression, and as I have stressed repeatedly, negative impressions can be difficult to reverse.

It is *your* responsibility to make sure that all of your application materials have arrived and are in your file by the deadline. It is not the responsibility of the graduate program staff to track down missing materials. Although some programs send postcards to applicants prior to the deadline, indicating the components that have or have not yet arrived, this is more of a courtesy than an obligation. An irritating tendency of some graduate school applicants is that they do not allow themselves enough time and then expect to receive some kind of special consideration when they miss a deadline. No matter what the excuse for being late is, they are unlikely to get much sympathy.

Even though most students aim to just meet the deadline date, there is really no reason why you should not be early, and there are many advantages to beating the deadline by a couple of weeks. For one thing, if you apply early you can wait patiently to receive confirmation that everything is in order, without losing any sleep over it. If for some reason a standardized test score or a transcript request is not processed properly, then you will still have time to correct the situation prior to the deadline. If you plan to beat an application deadline by a few weeks, then you are less likely to be rushing to get things together at the last moment. It is usually obvious from the quality of the application materials when students were disorganized and did not have enough time to do things properly.

Graduate Program Directors and secretaries don't like it when students call or drop by on the application deadline date, or perhaps a few days afterwards, and plead or insist on submitting an application, while promising that he or she will get all documentation in within the next week or so. Although many programs offer some leeway in accepting late applications, it is generally very difficult to obtain adequate documentation in time for a fair evaluation by the admissions committee. Trying to submit an application at this point is generally a waste of everyone's time!

There are additional reasons why you should try to get your application in a few weeks early: First, it will be noticed that you are well-organized. Second, you will appear to be enthusiastic about the program. Third, some programs actually begin reviewing applications before the deadline, even though most of them have not yet arrived. Application files that are reviewed early may receive a more careful evaluation. The more closely your application is looked over and the fewer competing applications there are at the time yours is evaluated, the more likely it is to stand out from the crowd.

Note that it is *not* a good idea to send individual items as you complete them with the idea that you are at least getting some parts of your application in early. Graduate program staff find it irritating to deal with items that trickle in one at a time, and there is more chance of something being misfiled or lost when this happens. You should only send in a complete application, unless other instructions are specified.

> *While it is advantageous to the applicant to submit an early application, one or two weeks early will suffice. There is no point in submitting an application <u>months</u> early. There can be a problem keeping track of the application and later in identifying it.*

The key to getting everything in on time with a minimum of stress and anxiety is to begin early. You need to begin taking the necessary steps well in advance of the application deadlines. Many students underestimate the amount of time involved in properly filling out application forms and writing a good personal statement or essay, the typical lags between when transcripts or standardized test scores are requested and when they actually arrive at their destinations, and the ideal amount of time that referees expect to have when asked for letters of recommendation. You need to make arrangements for things like transcripts, standardized test scores, and letters of recommendation several weeks prior to the deadlines. And in each instance you need to follow up at both ends, first to make sure that the materials have been sent, and later to make sure that they have been received.

If an international student is submitting an application, extra time over and above that suggested for North American students must be provided for receipt of all documentation, particularly transcripts and letters of recommendation.

In addition to these minimum time requirements, it is important to leave extra time in case any of the offices responsible for processing your requests make errors, or encounter technical delays. A transcript or standardized test score might not be sent out in a timely fashion because the original request was misplaced. It might be sent to the wrong address. A referee for one of your letters of recommendation might think your completed letter has been mailed, when it has really fallen behind her desk. Even the postal service is not perfect and things occasionally get lost in the mail. Any of these occurrences can cause significant delays in getting the required materials to their destination, and the program staff and admissions committees will not care to hear any excuses for why your application is incomplete.

You will note the various programs' application deadlines when you do your original research. I suggest that you make your request for application materials at least six months in advance of these deadlines. You should do so even sooner if you are going to be busy during the application period with a heavy course load or some other major time-consuming responsibility, or if you think that you will be applying for internal sources of funding from the program or university; the deadlines for applying for internal scholarships and other awards can sometimes precede the program application deadlines by a few months.

> *It is easy to understand why some programs flatly refuse to consider incomplete application files. Almost all programs receive many more applicants than they accept, and some of the more competitive programs receive more outstanding applicants with complete files than they can accept. Why should they consider applications that are incomplete when they don't have to go that far to fill their programs with excellent students?*

Keeping track of what you have done   As you begin filling out forms, requesting transcripts and letters of recommendation, etc., you will need to keep track of which things you have already taken care of for each application, and which things remain to be dealt with. You need some kind of filing and checklist system that will enable you to keep track of the requirements and deadlines of each program. You will use this checklist as you follow up to make sure that the programs receive your application materials on time. Keep track of every request you make for standardized test scores, transcripts, and letters of recommendation, the date that you made each request, and if applicable, the date that you receive confirmation that your request has been fulfilled.

Many programs will not inform you that they have received your application. Those that do so will vary a great deal in how long they wait to let you know. Some programs wait until all of the various components of your application have arrived — the application forms and other materials that you send, and the transcripts, standardized test scores, and letters of recommendation, all of which are coming from different places and will arrive at different times. If any of these have not arrived by the deadline, some programs will send a postcard telling you what is missing.

Make a photocopy of each complete application package prior to mailing it, and file these copies with your checklist. This will allow you to confirm what you have mailed in case there are problems with missing materials later on. If an application package does get lost or misdirected in the mail, you will have a backup copy to express mail or fax to the program in an emergency. Most importantly, you need to have a copy of everything you have sent in case you receive a phone call to discuss your application, or if you are invited for a pre-selection interview.

Another good reason to photocopy the package is just in case you don't get into the program you want the most, and you decide to reapply next year. Some programs will keep the files of unsuccessful applicants. If you reapply, you will want to make sure that your responses on application forms and in personal statements are consistent with the previous versions.

When you are finally ready to submit...   Unless a return envelope is provided with your application package, use one that is large enough so that you can mail your application materials flat. The program staff and admissions committee will find it easier to deal with a file that contains pages that lie flat. Use paper clips for attachments — not staples — as the program staff will want to organize the materials in their own preferred way, and they may wish to separate attachments from the application form or from each other.

Make a trip to the Post Office to mail your applications, rather than just dropping them in a mailbox. This way you can have them weighed so that you know you have used the correct first-class postage. It also eliminates some of the things that could possibly go wrong if you simply used the mailbox. For less than a dollar you can get a Certificate of Mailing from the Post Office in case you need to prove later that you sent something to a particular address on a particular date. It may be worth the extra few dollars to send your application by registered mail, just to make sure it is received at its destination.

Overnight couriers, such as Federal Express, are more expensive but they also offer secure and guaranteed timely delivery, and you might have no choice but to use them if you are sending material right at the deadline. But, keep in mind that an application that arrives by overnight courier can make one of two different impressions, depending on when it arrives relative to the deadline date: If it arrives a week or more before the deadline, it may be assumed that the applicant has the good judgment to send his or her application by a secured form of delivery. On the other hand, if it arrives right at the deadline, it may be assumed that the applicant was desperate and ran out of time because he or she was ill-prepared or otherwise disorganized.

When is it appropriate to call?   Because some programs do not inform students that their applications have been received, you may need to take steps to follow up on your own. It is reasonable to make a few prudent phone calls to a Graduate Program Director or secretary if confirmation of receipt does not come within a reasonable period of time. As long as you are not making repeated and frequent calls, you will not be seen as an anxious, neurotic pest. One or two brief, polite, and appropriately timed phone calls will indicate that you are merely taking proper responsibility for your application.

How long you should wait before calling to confirm that application materials have arrived depends upon which materials you are calling about. The application form and your personal statement or essays may be the only components of your application that you have direct responsibility for putting in the mail (unless the program requires you to collect your letters of recommendation and send them along with the application form). Expect it to take up to two weeks for your school to process your request to have transcripts mailed out. The testing service will take up to six weeks to process your request for standardized test scores and send them to the various graduate programs.

Not only do things take time to get to their destination after they are put in the mail, but it also takes time for the graduate program staff to organize and file incoming materials. Therefore, you should allow at least two or three weeks from the time that you mail an application to receive confirmation that it has been received.

Keep your calls brief, and do not complain or attempt to place blame if you are told that something is missing from your file that you are sure was mailed weeks ago. Make a promise to look into the matter from your end, and ask for suggestions of what else you can do in the meantime. Remain calm and polite at all times.

Follow up with those individuals who agreed to write letters of recommendation for you. Allow a couple of weeks after you solicit a letter of recommendation before calling your referees to check if they have remembered to mail your letter. Do not pressure them if they have not yet done so. Politely remind them of the approaching deadline and ask if they would mind if you called for confirmation in another week or two. If a referee confirms that a letter has already been mailed, record this on your checklist.

Missing documentation can be faxed to the program secretary and followed-up with delivery of the originals by courier, in person, or by regular mail. At the very least, submit a photocopy or fax of whatever documentation is missing. Then worry about getting the originals submitted, as soon as possible.

> *Despite the best efforts of applicants who do everything in their power to have all documentation arrive by the deadline, there can still be problems, particularly with nonreceipt of letters of recommendation that have either gone astray, or perhaps were never sent in the first place. It is not uncommon for professors to assure a student that a particular letter has been sent when in fact it was not.*

Summary   Many programs stick to their deadlines and will not consider an application if any of the required components are missing or late. It is your responsibility to make sure that all of your application materials have arrived and are in your file by the deadline. Don't make the mistake of assuming that because a document has been sent, it has also been received.

Organization is the key to dealing with multiple items for multiple application packages. Use a checklist to keep track of those things you have taken care of for each application, and which things remain to be dealt with. You need to follow up at each end, first to make sure that materials have been sent, and later to make sure they have been received.

Another key to getting everything in on time with a minimum of stress and anxiety is to begin early. Do not underestimate the amount of time involved in properly filling out application forms and writing a good personal statement or essay, the typical delay between when transcripts or standardized test scores are requested and when they actually arrive at their destinations, and the amount of time your referees will need to prepare your letters of recommendation.

There are several advantages to beating the application deadline by a couple of weeks: It may allow you enough time respond to unexpected problems that occur close to the deadline, such as unfulfilled requests for transcripts, test scores, or letters of recommendation. Getting your application in a couple of weeks before the deadline will also indicate that you are well-organized and enthusiastic about the program. Your application may receive a closer evaluation if the admissions committee begins reviewing files before the application deadline.

Make a photocopy of each complete application package prior to mailing it, and file these copies with your checklist. If an application package does get lost or misdirected in the mail, you will have a backup copy to send in an emergency. Also, you will want a copy of your application in case you are invited for a preselection interview. Mail your application materials flat, and use paper clips, not staples.

Wait at least three weeks from the time that you mail an application to receive confirmation that it has been received. If there is a problem, look into the matter from your end, and ask for suggestions of what else you can do. Remain calm and polite at all times.

Curriculum vitae and Résumés

You may or may not be required to submit with your application a résumé, or *curriculum vitae (c.v.)*, as they are referred to in academic circles. A résumé for graduate school is similar to a résumé that might accompany a typical job application. Like a job-seeker's résumé, the contents of an academic résumé or *c.v.* will depend on the purpose for which it is being used. In the case of your *c.v.* for graduate school application, it is a summary of your biographical features and a concise annotated history of what you have accomplished that is relevant to your qualifications and present interest in graduate school.

Who needs to prepare a c.v.?   Ask about *c.v.*s and résumés when you discuss graduate school with a professor or a career counsellor. Not everyone needs to put together a *c.v.*, but it is an absolute *must* in some fields. For applying to graduate school in most nonprofessional fields, you probably do not need to worry about putting together a *c.v.* if you have not yet done any relevant paid or volunteer work, if you do not belong to any professional organizations, if you have not contributed to any published scientific, literary, or artistic works, and if you have never won any academic awards.

If you have already accomplished more than one of these things, then you should consider starting your *c.v.* I use the word "starting" here because after you compile your *c.v.* the first time, you will want to continue to update it a couple of times each year while you are a graduate student. Do not feel bad if there is not very much to put in your *c.v.* right now. This is normal for students in most fields who are applying to their first graduate program.

Even when it is not explicitly required, there are several ways that a *c.v.* can be a useful tool and even though you don't have to submit a *c.v.*, you might want to include one with your application under certain circumstances. The usual caution against submitting more than the requested materials does not apply as strongly to an unsolicited *c.v.* as it does to other materials. Most admission committees would

---

This book uses the terms <u>curriculum</u> <u>vita</u> and <u>résumé</u> interchangeably because most people do so, even though the terms actually refer to different things. A curriculum vita is a comprehensive biographical statement emphasizing professional qualifications and activities, whereas a résumé is a custom-designed summary of one's qualifications that is intended to demonstrate suitability for a particular position or type of position. A résumé is usually much shorter than a c.v. because it focuses on only the individual's strongest qualifications.

appreciate seeing one as long as it is done properly, mainly because a *c.v.* can make it easier for them to evaluate you.

For a majority of students, the most important use for their *c.v.* is not as a supplement to the rest of their application materials, but rather as an information resource for the referees who write their letters of recommendation, and for prospective supervisors during preapplication correspondence, a topic that will be dealt with later in this chapter.

> *Do not try to make up for a sparse c.v. by including irrelevant information or wordy descriptions. This will only annoy the reader and reflect badly on your judgment. If you do not feel that putting together your c.v. at this time is justified because you have not yet accomplished much, then you may be better off to just work on an interesting and informative cover letter.*

The format and content of your c.v.   The appropriate content of a *c.v.* depends on the stage that people are at in their career, the nature of their past accomplishments, and on the purpose for which the vitae will be utilized. For example, the *c.v.* of a professor who is applying for a research grant might emphasize his or her publication record and previously awarded grants, whereas that of a senior undergraduate applying for graduate school would probably emphasize fieldwork or other relevant experience, information that may have no place in the professor's vitae.

There are some general norms with respect to formatting résumés or curriculum vitae. For instance, the items in each section should be listed in either chronological order or reverse-chronological order. Whichever mode of ordering the material you choose, use the same one for every section. Which sections are best to emphasize, and which additional ones might be included, depends on the field of study. A professor in your department or a career counsellor might be able to help you with this. The *Resources* section has information on some general guidebooks for preparing a *c.v.*

Biographical Information.   This should be the first section of any *c.v.* It includes information such as your name, address, birth-date, birthplace, and country of citizenship. Some information is optional, such as your sex, marital status, or number of dependents. Other biographical information is simply inappropriate, such as your religion, or sexual preferences.

Educational History.   Usually, this should be the second section. Your *relevant* educational history began after you finished high school. Therefore, the year that you graduated from high school should be the earliest item listed; it will be either the first item or the last item, depending on whether you are listing things in chronological or reverse-chronological order. This section should include all higher educational institutions you have attended, such as colleges, universities, trade schools, etc. List any degrees or diplomas that you obtained and the month and year in which they were conferred. List your major field of study and your minor, if applicable.

Relevant Work and Other Experience.   List any paid or volunteer work related to your proposed field of study. Give the name of your position, if applicable, and a *brief* description of your duties and responsibilities. Provide the name of the employer, location, and name and phone number of your supervisor, if applicable. Your previous job as a french fries chef at a fast-food restaurant is not relevant. On the other hand, if you held a managerial position at the restaurant, then this could be relevant. In the latter case, you would have to make sure that the managerial nature of your position was obvious to people reading your résumé so that they would not assume "french fries chef" when they noticed that you worked at a fast-food restaurant.

Special Skills.   In this section, provide a brief description of any special skills you possess. Examples include computer skills, whether they be programming abilities or simply familiarity with particular software packages. Do you possess specific analytical skills? Writing or public-speaking skills? Include a brief reference to some evidence that you do indeed possess these skills. For example, you might refer to a job you had as a lab assistant where you wrote a program that was used in an experiment.

Publications and presentations.   Most students who are applying to their first graduate degree program have little, if anything, to put in this section. As usual, the norms depend on the field of study. Use the designation "in preparation" if a manuscript pertaining to a project on which you will be author or a co-author is currently being written for publication. Use the designation "submitted for publication" if the manuscript is currently under peer review or editorial review, and "in press," if it has been accepted by a publisher but is not yet in print.

Honors and Awards.   For the most part, this section should be limited to academic honors and awards that you have obtained since finishing high school. In most cases, you should not refer to similar accomplishments from high school, as this will make your *c.v.* appear sophomoric. Exceptions might be made for truly outstanding honors, such as being a class Valedictorian or a Merit Scholar.

Membership in professional associations, societies, organizations, or other relevant groups.   Provide the name of the association or society, and the month and year that you became a member.

References.   The final section should provide the names, titles, addresses, and telephone and fax numbers of three or four references. Make sure that you ask these individuals for permission to list them as references. Do not assume that someone who agreed to write a letter of recommendation for you is also willing to be a long-term reference listed in your curriculum vitae.

The appearance of your c.v.   As usual, appearances are important. You want your *c.v.* to look professional. Proofread it carefully to make sure there are no typos or grammatical errors. Use a consistent format for your section headings and, as much as possible, for the content of information under each heading. If you are making photocopies to submit to referees or to prospective supervisors, make sure the copies are clean.

Your résumé should be easy to read. Readability is enhanced by using appropriate spaces between the various sections and subsections. The text within each section should be single-spaced. All four page margins (top, bottom, left, and right hand margins), should be three-quarters of an inch to one inch. Many readers will appreciate having enough space in the margins and between sections that they can write their own notes or comments directly on your *c.v.*, if they have their own copy. You should not try to compensate for a sparse résumé by using unnecessarily wide spaces and margins. Again, it just shows poor judgment and it will not fool anyone into thinking that you have a more extensive background.

> *A c.v. will only be helpful to the admissions committee if it does what it is supposed to do — it should provide a concise, easy-to-read summary of the most important information about you. But in order for it to be truly effective, you need to make it more than a simple documentation of biographical data and past accomplishments. You must treat it as an important promotional document — one that is designed to SELL the product that it describes, which of course is YOU.*

Summary   Your academic résumé or *c.v.* is a summary of your biographical features and a concise annotated history of what you have accomplished that is relevant to your qualifications and current interest in graduate school.

Not everyone needs to put together a *c.v.*, but it is an absolute *necessity* in some fields of study. Find out the norms for your field by asking a professor or career counsellor. You may not need to worry about a *c.v.* if you have not yet done any relevant paid or volunteer work, do not belong to any professional organizations, have not contributed to any published scientific, literary, or artistic works, and have never won any academic awards.

The most important use that graduate school applicants have for a *c.v.* is as an information resource for the referees who write their letters of recommendation, and for prospective supervisors during preapplication correspondence.

The items in each section should be listed in either chronological order or reverse-chronological order. Appropriate categories of information for most graduate school résumés include: a) biographical information, b) educational history, c) relevant work and other experience, d) special skills, e) publications and presentations, f) honors and awards, g) membership in professional associations, societies, organizations, or other relevant groups, and h) a short list of personal references.

The appearance of your résumé or *c.v.* suggests certain things about you. Make it look professional. Make sure there are no typos or grammatical errors. It should be easy to read, which requires proper use of margins and spacing. Do not try to make up for a sparse *c.v.* or résumé by including irrelevant information or wordy descriptions. This will only annoy the reader and reflect badly on your judgment.

<u>READ FINANCIAL-AID INFORMATION CAREFULLY!</u>

Financial-aid applications may come as part of the program application package, or else as a separate package from the campus financial aid office. There may be separate applications for loans and scholarships. You may have to send forms directly to the school, or to a central processing agency. Do not miss deadlines, as they are used to reduce the pool of applicants for limited funding.

Chapter 10

Putting It All Together
For a Winning Application

Overcoming Psychological Challenges

The process of applying to graduate school presents most students with a number of psychological challenges. You may experience doubts about your qualifications as you research various graduate programs. You may feel awkward while soliciting letters of recommendation from professors. You may be overcome with anxiety as you try to write your personal statement, or with boredom as you spend hours filling out tedious application forms.

Not only do these emotions feel uncomfortable, but they can also cause procrastination when it comes to initiating or completing essential tasks. I cannot counsel you on how to overcome procrastination, other than to refer you to a book: *The Now Habit: A Strategic Program For Overcoming Procrastination and Enjoying Play,* by N.A. Fiore; additional reference information is provided in the *Resources* section (General Advisement Guides). There are other self-help books on overcoming procrastination, but Fiores' book is as good as any I have ever seen on this topic.

Someone whose judgment you trust, perhaps a professor or a career counsellor, might suggest that because of your mediocre grades you do not have a realistic chance of getting into graduate school. You might be disheartened to hear someone voice a doubtful opinion of your chances, but you should not put too much stock into only one person's opinion. Someone's low estimation of your chances of getting into a graduate program may be based on the assumption that you will approach the application process the way that most students do. If this were true, then perhaps your chances of getting in *would* be slim. But, that is not the approach you are going to take. You are going to do things to set yourself apart from the typical applicant.

Many students wage a fierce battle with self-doubt throughout the application process. Still, it is easy to see why this happens, and books like this one can be part of the problem! We have discussed a great number of factors that could potentially play some role in determining the fate of your graduate school or professional school application. Based on this information and advice, one could, in principle, imagine the perfect applicant. Many students compare themselves to this imaginary *perfect* applicant, and feel despondent upon realizing that they don't measure up in all respects. Reality does not usually justify this concern because no applicants have everything going their way like the fantasy applicant does — not even those who will eventually be accepted into the most competitive programs in their field.

Armed with the information and advice in this book, you are now prepared to take the necessary steps to set yourself apart from the typical applicant. But first, you need some measure of self-confidence that you can do it. Without this confidence, most students won't even begin the process of applying to graduate school. If self-doubt is a problem area for you, then you will find that after you have a detailed plan of action down on paper, as discussed later in this chapter, the much needed sense of confidence and control will begin to emerge.

Avoid costly mistakes after the application deadline   One of the most formidable psychological challenges comes after you have done all that you need to do. The application deadline is past, and you have confirmed that your file is complete at each of the programs to which you have applied. Decisions won't be announced for several more weeks. The wait may seem unbearable, and you may find yourself having all sorts of irrational ideas about what might be going on.

Is it true what you have heard others say — "No news is good news?" Or have the selections already been made and the program forgot to inform you? Should you just call and find out what's going on?

It is understandable that there would be some anxiety while you wait out this period, but you must not let it cause you to act impulsively. Resist all temptation to call and ask about the status of your application or how the admissions committee is coming along with their selections. An exception could be made if a program had informed you about a decision date that has already passed by more than a week without a word. In some cases, however, you may actually hurt your chances of a favorable decision on your application by calling about these things. Such a call might be perceived as an attempt to manipulate the decision makers. Or it could give the impression that you are egocentric, imagining your candidacy is of monumental importance to the program. Or it could suggest that you are impulsive or neurotic. If someone from a program wants to talk with you about your application, that person will call you.

Applicants to graduate school often overlook the influence that the graduate program secretary can have on how their application is processed. Yet they are likely to end up speaking with this person every time they call the program about something. This important staff member plays a critical role in the admissions procedure, as he or she will be responsible for receiving and sorting all of the application materials into separate files, and assisting the admissions committee or other faculty members in dealing with all of the information.

Whenever applicants call to ask about something, the graduate program secretary will try to find the answer — unless, of course, the caller is overbearing or rude. The program secretaries can be helpful friends, or significant foes. You do not want to annoy these individuals. Treat them with the respect they deserve, and do not pester them with inappropriate calls and inquiries.

Making and Following a Plan

This book contains a great deal of advice that you can use to improve your chances of being accepted into the right graduate or professional school. But most of it will be of limited use to you if you fall victim to one of the greatest pitfalls — a lack of sufficient planning. Most first-time graduate school applicants drastically underestimate the amount of time required to complete all of the application requirements. If you are serious about your desire to get into graduate school, you must take a serious approach to devising and implementing an organized strategy.

You have already taken the first and most important step — you have read through this book and you now have a better understanding of what graduate school is all about and how the selection of graduate school applicants really works. No doubt you already have several ideas of how you could improve your own chances of getting into the program you want. However, all the reading and thinking in the world won't do you any good if you cannot put what you have learned into action. This is the most difficult part. Execution of an effective application strategy will involve tremendous effort. The enthusiasm that comes with new ideas might help you get started, but the really hard part will be to continually act on those ideas until your mission is completed.

Now that you have read this book, the next step is also very important: You should take the time to sit down and write out a plan of action for yourself. This means, literally, *write* a plan. It does not need to be much more than a list of points — things that you will set out to accomplish between now and when you send out your applications. Any successful business person or entrepreneur will tell you that good ideas and opportunities are hard to capitalize on without first having a plan.

Going through the exercise of writing out a plan forces you to think practically about specific objectives and about the steps you will take to accomplish them. It also enables you to see how the advice and recommendations in this book fit with your own situation. There will be a lot of little things you wish to accomplish. By listing them together, you will have a better overall picture of what you must do. This overall plan is essential to avoid getting off track as you work toward your goal.

After listing your objectives, state exactly how you will accomplish each one. It is a good idea at this point to put a time-frame on things. This will help you to avoid pitfalls that could arise unexpectedly when you try to implement your plan. After you have written out your plan, put it somewhere handy so you can consult it often to make sure you are still on track.

You will find that occasionally referring back to your plan of action will reveal ways of improving it, or at least ways to be more specific in how to accomplish your particular objectives. Situations will change, opportunities will appear, others will disappear. You need to continually refer to your plan as you are implementing it so that you can update and change it as you go along. You want to remain organized, yet flexible in your approach. It is worth noting that these two qualities — organization and flexibility — are hallmarks of most successful graduate students. So start incorporating them into your behavioral repertoire now!

A sample plan and timetable   I hope that you are reading this book while you are still at least a year away from applying to graduate school. This is simply because it is so important that you start your preparations early. Ideally, your planning should begin right from when you start undergraduate school!

Unfortunately, it's more likely that most students who read this book won't do so until they are only one semester away from applying, or perhaps even *while* they are dealing with applications. There are still a number of things that late-starters can do to improve their chances, but they will need to establish priorities that are somewhat different than those of the early-starters. They will have to do some things on a different schedule.

The following step-by-step timetable should help you plan your own course of action. Keep in mind that not all aspects of this idealized plan will be appropriate for applying to all programs. Note also that making full use of some of the recommendations requires that initial steps be initiated at certain general points in time before applying to graduate school. Exactly how much you can do beyond what you have already accomplished will depend mostly on how much time you have before you will be applying. If you are starting late, you will probably have to cut some corners. A few of the recommended steps may have to be sacrificed, or implemented so quickly that they can't be done perfectly. Some of the recommended steps are not essential, whereas others are so important that you will have no choice but to take them.

A number of assumptions were made in compiling the following plan and timetable: First, they are suggested for undergraduates who will be applying to their first graduate program, to begin in the semester after they finish undergraduate school. Many of the steps, and certain aspects of the timing, will not make sense for a master's student who expects to be applying to a doctoral program.

Second, it is based on a typical four-year undergraduate program, so students who are enrolled in a program of a different duration will have to make some adjustments, especially for the earlier parts of the plan.

Finally, the timetable assumes that your earliest application deadline is February 1. Obviously, you will need to make adjustments if your earliest application deadline is more than a few weeks before or after February 1, especially for the later parts of the plan.

Remember, there are probably very few students who can implement the following plan exactly and according to the suggested timetable. Do not be distressed if you get the feeling that you didn't begin your planning early enough. Most of those applicants with whom you will be competing will not have done so either. Use the sample plan as a guideline for making your own action plan. (The chapters which discuss particular points in more detail are provided in parentheses).

During Your Freshman and Sophomore Academic Years

___Visit the career counsellors on your campus. Ask for help in learning about the kinds of careers that are available for people with the baccalaureate degree you are seeking, and those that are available to individuals with an advanced degree. Consult books and guides on career options, starting with those listed in the *Resources* section. Find out early whether graduate school is necessary for your general career aspirations. (chapter 3)

___Find out what courses you will need to take for your major, and which ones are especially important for students wishing to go to graduate school afterwards. (chapter 6)

___Plan the tentative sequence of courses you will take for your major over the remainder of your undergraduate career. Do not plan to take all of the toughest courses in your senior year, as you will need much time during that period to deal with your graduate school applications. In most circumstances, and to the extent that it is possible, it is best to plan to take your most difficult required courses during your junior year.

___Start a folder to contain all of the syllabi for courses you will take during the remainder of your undergraduate career. This will be a precious time-saver later on if you need to provide details about your academic background.

___Begin to attend events sponsored by your department (guest lectures, colloquia, symposia, exhibits, shows, socials, etc.). Get into the habit of checking the department bulletin boards for news. (chapter 5)

___Start getting to know some of your professors personally. Let them know that you plan to go to graduate school and why. You will need to find opportunities to speak with professors outside of class, but don't pester them with frequent uninvited visits to their offices. (chapter 5)

___Join any applicable student organizations or associations in your major field of study.

Note that although there is some important planning to do during the freshman and sophomore years, your *main* task during this time is to concentrate on your study skills so that you obtain the best grades in your coursework that you can.

During Your Junior Academic Year (first half)

____Generally, the junior year should be when you take your most demanding courses. It is a good idea to find out during the summer what textbooks you will need for your first-semester courses and start reading *before* school starts.

____If you haven't already done so, this is the time to make definite decisions about the career you want to pursue (you can always change your mind and your plans someday down the road). Find out everything you can about what this type of career involves. Find out if there is a mentorship program at your school that you can join. (chapter 3)

____Talk to seniors in your major field who are on the graduate school track. Ask them what they have learned about various graduate programs and the graduate school application process (You may discover that you are better informed than they are, in which case you might want to recommend this book to them!). Ask them about their experiences with soliciting support from faculty members in your department.

____Begin networking with graduate students in your department, if there are any. The best way to start may be to talk with the teaching assistants for your professors' courses, as most T.A.s are also graduate students. (chapter 3)

____Learn about the research and/or other interests of the various faculty in your department. Visit with one or more who seem to be well-matched to your own interests and volunteer to help them. Let them know about your graduate school plans. (chapter 5)

____Start to get acquainted with the directories, Internet web sites, etc., which describe graduate programs in your field of interest. (Resources)

____Note what time of year seniors in your major field are dealing with their graduate school applications. Late fall and early winter are common periods for this as graduate programs in many disciplines have application deadlines between the beginning of January and the end of March. Keep in mind that a majority of students will have started later than they should have. If you know someone who is dealing with applications, ask if you can examine the materials. (chapter 3)

___Check with an undergraduate advisor in your department or with the Registrar's office to make sure you are still on the right track for fulfilling your graduation requirements next year.

During Your Junior Academic Year (second half)

___Take courses taught by professors whose interests are most in line with yours. Put all you can into these courses as you will probably be asking these professors for letters of recommendation next year. (chapter 7)

___Research the financial-aid opportunities. Remember that application deadlines for many scholarships come long before you will be applying to graduate programs. (chapter 3)

___Early in this semester you should begin looking for summer job opportunities in your field. Don't wait until the semester is almost over, or someone else may beat you to the best opportunities. (chapter 5)

___This semester may also be a good time to start preparing for any standardized tests you will need to write. If you write these tests during the late spring or in the summer, then you may have an opportunity to rewrite in the event that you do poorly the first time. If you decide not to write your standardized tests until the late summer or fall, then you should delay most of your preparation until this semester is over so that you can concentrate on your coursework. (chapter 6)

___Look up some of the general advisement guides and other books listed in the *Resources* section.

___Check with professors whom you are likely to ask for letters of recommendation next year to make sure that they expect to be on campus then. Remember that some professors may be on sabbatical leave, in retirement, or moving to a different locale and unavailable to write letters for you. (chapter 7)

___Make a preliminary draft of your résumé or *c.v.*, if you plan to use one. (chapter 9)

During the Summer Before Your Senior Year

___The summer prior to your senior year should be spent at a job or in volunteer work that will provide you with relevant experience related to the field in which you will be doing graduate work. Make sure that you also have time during the summer to deal with the following steps:

___Continue to research the graduate programs in your field and the faculty in those programs.

___You should have a good idea of where you most want to go to graduate school by the time your senior academic year begins. If you can afford it, try to visit those programs that interest you the most. (chapter 4)

___Make your tentative list of programs to apply to and request their application packages before the end of summer. You may narrow down your list of prospective programs later. (chapter 5)

___If you will be applying to programs where you will have a graduate supervisor, then establish personal contact with the relevant faculty members in those programs and with their current graduate students, if they have any. (chapters 4 and 8)

___Prepare for standardized tests if you haven't already written them, or if you will be rewriting during the fall. (chapter 6)

During Your Senior Academic Year

Things will start to speed up after the summer ends, and your planning should now be on a monthly or even weekly basis. If it is not necessary to take a full course load in both semesters of your senior year, try to keep your load as light as possible during the first semester, when you will be dealing with the most hectic part of the application process. It is better to have a heavier course load in the second semester when you are already done with most of the application work.

September

___Organize the application packages you've requested as they begin to arrive, with a separate folder for each program. (chapter 6)

___If possible, take an additional course taught by professors with whom you have taken an earlier course, and whom you will be asking for a letter of recommendation. (chapter 7)

___Start to put together a package to give to your referees to help them write effective letters for you. Order a copy of your transcripts, and make photocopies to include in this package. (chapter 7)

___Contact the financial aid offices at the schools on your list and ask for information about the aid available to graduate students. (chapter 3)

October

___Finalize the list of programs to which you will apply.

___Note whether any of the programs require submission of financial-assistance forms prior to the program application deadlines. (chapter 3)

___Find out if there are any workshops or short courses at your school aimed at helping students deal with graduate school applications. Various departments and students' associations run these helpful courses during the fall.

___Begin brainstorming about your personal statements or essays. Remember that you should probably spend a couple of weeks preparing ideas before you actually begin writing. (chapter 7)

___Order official transcripts to be sent to the programs to which you are applying. If you wrote your standardized tests earlier, arrange with the testing service to have your official scores sent to the right programs. Remember that these requests must be made at least six weeks prior to the programs' application deadlines. If you wait until December to order transcripts and test scores for a February 1 deadline, you will have to hope that those individuals fulfilling your orders do everything right. It is wiser to play it safe by making your requests an extra four to six weeks earlier. (chapter 9)

November

___Request letters of recommendation from your referees. (chapter 7)

___Begin writing your personal statements or essays. (chapter 7)

___Confirm that your school sent the transcripts you requested last month. (chapter 9)

December

___Finish your personal statements or essays if you haven't already done so. Get feedback prior to preparing your final drafts. (chapter 7)

___Fill out application forms. (chapter 6)

___Work on your application cover letter, if one is needed. (chapter 8)

Christmas break

___Send your applications now so they arrive a few weeks before the application deadline. (Remember, this sample timetable assumes a February 1 deadline). Make photocopies of all the materials in each application package before you mail them. (chapter 9)

___The grades you received in courses that you just finished were not included in your earlier transcripts. Order transcripts for these courses now and have them sent to the programs to which you are applying. (chapter 9)

___If you have time over the holidays, and if you can afford it, make an effort to visit any interesting programs that you weren't able to visit during the previous summer. (chapter 4)

___If you are applying to programs that conduct preselection interviews, start planning now to make sure that you will have the money you need to attend an interview in the spring, if you happen to be invited for one. (chapter 7)

January

___This is the time for following up, and correcting any last-minute deficiencies. Check with your referees to see if they have sent your letters of recommendation. Call the programs to make sure your applications have arrived and are complete. (chapter 9)

___You may need to apply for student loans at this time if you think you will need this form of financial aid when graduate school begins in the fall. (chapter 3)

___Once you have confirmed that everything is in order with all of your applications, you should probably try to forget about them for a couple of weeks and just concentrate on any coursework you have ongoing. All matters concerning your applications are out of your hands at this point, and you may need some distractions to help deal with any undue anxiety you have about this. (Review the section in this chapter on avoiding costly mistakes after the application deadline).

February

___If you have applied to programs that conduct preselection interviews, start preparing in case you are invited for one. (chapter 7)

Congratulations! You have completed the application process. If you have been careful in selecting programs, if your academic credentials indicate that you have intellectual potential, and if your referees are convinced that you have what it takes to succeed in graduate school, then you should feel optimistic about your chances of getting into a graduate program that is right for you. I sincerely wish you a successful application and a rewarding graduate education. You are about to embark on a path to greater freedom to pursue your interests and make your own choices. Good luck!

Resources

There are many useful guides, directories, and books to help students prepare for graduate school application. A partial listing of these follows. Many are available in the reference section of your college library, or from a career counsellor.

If you wish to purchase a copy of any book directly from its publisher, you will find addresses, telephone numbers, and fax numbers for almost every publishing company in the U.S. and Canada by looking in *Literary Market Place*, which can be found in the reference section of almost any library.

Contents

CAREER OPTIONS

Major Options: The Student's Guide to Linking College Majors and Career Opportunities During and After College. Basta, Nicholas. New York, NY: Harper Collins, 1991.

Describes the 30 most popular majors in the U.S., including courses of study, workload, and lists of numerous careers to which they may lead.

Occupational Outlook Handbook. 1994-95 ed. Washington, DC: United States Department of Labor, 1994.

Provides descriptions of occupations, detailing the nature of the work, working conditions, employment, training/qualifications, job outlook, earnings, and related occupations. Published every two years.

Canada's Best Careers Guide. Feather, Frank. 3rd ed. Toronto, ON: Warwick, 1994.

Written by one of Canada's leading business futurists. Feather presents his ideas on the Canadian job market of the future, both by industry group and career.

Job Futures/Emplois-avenir. 1996 ed. Ottawa, ON: Employment and Immigration Canada, 1996.

A two-volume set available in English or French. Provides information on 211 occupational groups, listing current labor-market conditions, salaries and employment projections. It also details the job prospects for graduates of 155 postsecondary programs of academic study. Also on the Internet: [www.hrc-drhc.gc.ca/hrdc/corp/stratpol/jobs]

National Occupational Classification/Classification nationale des professions. Ottawa, ON: Minister of Supply and Services, 1993.

Two-volume Canadian government publication, available in English or French. Profiles thousands of occupations.

Where the Jobs Are: Career Survival for Canadians in the New Global Economy. Campbell, Colin. Toronto, ON: MacFarlane Walter & Ross, 1996.

Explores the global job market, indicating which countries, industries, and companies show the greatest potential.

What Color Is Your Parachute: A Practical Manual for Job-Hunters & Career Changers. Bolles, Richard. 1997 ed. Berkeley, CA: Ten Speed Press, 1997.

A must-read for all job hunters and those considering a career change. Updated annually. French and Spanish translations available. Includes excellent bibliographies.

GRADUATE PROGRAM DIRECTORIES

What follows are two selective lists of graduate program directories. The first section provides information on directories with a multi-subject approach, and the second section lists directories for specific subject areas.

A word to the wise — do not rely on just one directory when compiling lists of programs. It is always a good idea to use several sources to ensure that your list is as comprehensive as possible.

General Directories

College Blue Book. 25th ed. New York: Macmillan, 1995.

A 5-volume set which provides information on undergraduate and graduate programs. It is primarily American with selective information on Canadian schools. It is particularly useful for its specific program headings. For example, one can find programs such as glassblowing, insurance & risk management, peace studies, and medical illustration.

Official GRE CGS Directory of Graduate Programs. 15th ed. Princeton, NJ: Educational Testing Service, 1995.

A 4-volume set which not only has an arrangement by program but also provides the following information in tabular format: admission and degree requirements, enrolment and faculty numbers, tuition and housing expenses, and financial aid information. It is primarily American, but includes information on some Canadian schools.

Peterson's Annual Guides to Graduate Study, 1996. 31st ed. Princeton, NJ: Peterson's Guides, 1997.

This 6-volume set provides a wealth of information on programs, including admission requirements, deadline dates, degree require-ments, financial aid, expenses, etc. Also available in CD-Rom and on the Internet.

- Peterson's Guides to Graduate & Professional Programs, Bk.1: An Overview 1997 31st ed., Lefferts, A. (Editor). Peterson's Guides.

- Peterson's Guide to Graduate Programs in Business, Education, Health & Law 1997, 31st ed. Peterson's Guides.

- Peterson's Guide to Graduate Programs in Engineering and Applied Sciences 1997, 31st ed. Peterson's Guides.

- Peterson's Guide to Graduate Programs in the Biological & Agricultural Sciences 1997, 31st ed. Peterson's Guides.

- Peterson's Guide to Graduate Programs in the Humanities, Arts, and Social Sciences 1997, 31st ed. Peterson's Guides.

- Peterson's Guide to Graduate Programs in the Physical Sciences and Mathematics 1997, 31st ed. Peterson's Guides.

Canadian Professional Schools Factsheets. Purcell, Catherine. 1996-98 ed. Toronto, ECW Press, 1996.

Provides information on admission requirements and application details for professional programs such as architecture, journalism, law, library science, dentistry, medicine, nursing, occupational therapy, physical therapy, social work, teacher education, and veterinary medicine.

Directory of Canadian Universities/Répertoire des universités canadiennes. 30th ed. Ottawa, ON: Association of Universities and Colleges of Canada, 1996.

Lists graduate and undergraduate degrees by subject. University profiles outline information of a general nature. No details are provided on the individual programs themselves.

National Guide to College and University Programmes/Répertoire national des programmes des collèges et des universités. Ottawa, ON: Human Resources Development Canada, 1995.

Useful for its very specific subject headings. For example, one can locate programs such as jazz studies, kinesiology, costume studies, and soil science.

Subject Directories

This section covers directories that focus on a specific subject area. If you do not find what you are looking for here, go to your library or a career counsellor for help finding the information you need. The directories listed here cover American and Canadian schools unless otherwise indicated.

Audiology and Speech Pathology

Guide to Graduate Education in Speech-Language Pathology and Audiology. 1991-1992 ed. Rockville, MD: American Speech-Language-Hearing Association, 1991.

Includes only U.S. schools.

Biology

Graduate Programs in Animal Behavior in the United States, Canada, Mexico. 5th ed. Omaha, NE: Creighton University Department of Biology, 1990.

Business

Barron's Guide to Graduate Business Schools. Miller, Eugene. 9th ed. Hauppauge, NY: Barron's Educational Series, 1995.

Guide to Doctoral Programs in Business & Management. Soete, Catherine J., (Editor) St. Louis, MO: American Assembly of Collegiate Schools of Business, 1995.

Guide to MBA Programs in Canada, 1995-97.   Purcell, Catherine. 3rd ed. Toronto, ECW Press, 1995.

Includes only Canadian schools.

The Official Guide to MBA Programs, 1994-96.   8th ed. Princeton, NJ: Graduate Management Admission Council, 1996.

The Official Guide to MBA Programs, Krasna, J.Z. (Editor). 7th ed. 1994, (ISBN 0-446-39559-5) Warner Books, Inc. (Special Sales Dept. phone 212-522-7381).

Where to Study Public Relations - A Student's Guide to Academic Programs in the U.S. and Canada.   New York: Public Relations Society of America, 1997.

Which MBA?   A Critical Guide to the World's Best Programmes. Bickerstaffe, George. 6th ed. Don Mills, ON: Addison-Wesley, 1994.

Chemistry

Chemical Sciences Graduate School Finder, 1996-1997. 6th ed. Washington, DC: American Chemical Society, 1996.

Graduate and Post-Doctoral Training Programs in Clinical Chemistry. Washington, DC: American Association for Clinical Chemistry, 1991.

Communication Studies

The Communication Disciplines in Higher Education: A Guide to Academic Programs in the United States and Canada. Elmore, Garland C., (Editor) 2nd ed. Murray, KY: Association for Communication Administration, 1993.

Computer Science

The Complete Guide to Animation and Computer Graphics Schools. Pintoff, Ernest. New York: Watson-Guptill, 1995.

Criminology and Police Work

Graduate Programs: Master of Science in Forensic Science. Colorado Springs, CO: American Academy of Forensic Sciences (undated).

Includes only U.S. schools.

Dentistry

Admission Requirements of U.S. and Canadian Dental Schools, 1997-98. 34th ed. Washington, DC: American Association of Dental Schools, 1995.

Education-Administration

Directory of Graduate Preparation Programs in College Student Personnel. Alexandria, VA: American College Personnel Association, 1990.

Engineering

Directory of Engineering Graduate Studies & Research. Washington, DC: American Society for Engineering Education, 1993.

Environmental Studies

Canadian Graduate Programs in Environmental Studies. 1996-1997 ed. Kingston, ON: Queen's University School of Environmental Studies, 1996.

Includes only Canadian schools.

Geography

Guide to Programs in Geography in the United States and Canada, 1995-96. 28th ed. Washington, DC: Association of American Geographers, 1995.

Guidance and Counselling

Counselor Preparation, 1996-98: Programs, Personnel, Trends. Hollis, Joseph W. 9th ed. Muncie, IN: Accelerated Development, 1996.

Includes only U.S. schools.

History

Directory of History Departments and Organizations in the United States and Canada. 20th ed. 1994-95. Washington, DC: American Historical Association, 1994.

Handbook to Graduate Programmes in History in Canada/Guide des programmes d'études supérieures en histoire au Canada. Calverley, David, and Stadfeld, Bruce, eds. Ottawa, ON: Graduate Students' Committee of the Canadian Historical Association, 1994.

Includes only Canadian schools.

Humanities

Directory of Programs in Linguistics in the United States & Canada, 1995. 9th ed. Washington, DC: Linguistic Society of America, 1994.

Graduate and Post-Doctoral Programs in Bioethics and Medical Humanities. Minneapolis, MN: University of Minnesota, 1994.

Includes only U.S. schools.

Institution and Service Management

Guide to Arts Administration Training, 1993-94. Prieve, E. Arthur, (Editor) New York, NY: American Council for the Arts, 1993.

Health Services Administration Education: Directory of Programs 1996-98. Dickens, Martha, (Editor) 10th ed. Arlington, VA: Association of University Programs in Health Administration, 1996.

Your Career As a Healthcare Executive, 1995-96: A Profile of the Profession Including a List of the Accredited Graduate Programs. Chicago, IL: American College of Healthcare Executives, 1995.

Interdisciplinary Studies

Graduate and Undergraduate Programs and Courses in Middle East Studies in the United States, Canada, and Abroad. Tucson, AZ: Middle East Studies Association of North America, 1993.

Guide to Graduate Work in Women's Studies. Humphreys, Debra, (Editor) College Park, MD: National Women's Studies Association, 1991.

Includes only U.S. schools.

Guide to International Studies at Canadian Universities/ Guide pour les études internationales aux universitiés canadiennes. Ottawa, ON: Association of Universities and Colleges of Canada, 1993.

Includes only Canadian schools.

National Directory of Educational Programs in Gerontology and Geriatrics. Lobenstine, Joy C., (Editor) 5th ed. Washington, DC: Association for Gerontology in Higher Education, 1991.

Programs and Courses in Gerontology and Geriatrics in Post-Secondary Institutions in Canada/Programmes et cours en gérontologie et gériatrie en établissements post-secondaires au Canada. Ottawa, ON: Canadian Association of Gerontology, 1994.

Includes only Canadian schools.

Law

Guide to Law Schools in Canada, 1996-97. Purcell, Catherine. Toronto, ON: ECW Press, 1996.

Includes only Canadian schools.

Official Guide to U.S. Law Schools. 1997 edition. New York, NY: Bantam Doubleday Dell, 1996.

Includes only U.S. schools.

Library Science

Graduate Library Education Programs: Accredited by the American Library Association Under Standards for Accreditation. Chicago, IL: American Library Association, 1993.

Medicine and Genetics

Directory of Graduate Medical Education Programs, 1992-1993.   78th ed.   Chicago, IL: American Medical Association, 1992.

Includes only U.S. schools.

Guide to North American Graduate and Postgraduate Training Programs in Human Genetics, 1996-97.   6th ed. Bethesda, MD: American Society of Human Genetics, 1996.

Medical School Admission Requirements, 1997-1998. 47th ed. Washington, DC: Association of American Medical Colleges, 1996.

M.S. and Ph.D. Programs in Medical Physics.   College Park, MD: American Association of Physicists in Medicine, 1994.

Meteorology and Climatology

Curricula in the Atmospheric, Oceanic, Hydrologic, and Related Sciences: Colleges and Universities in the United States, Canada, and Puerto Rico. Boston, MA: American Meteorological Society, 1994.

Museum Studies

Museum Studies Programs in Canada/Programmes de formation museologique au Canada. Ottawa, ON: Canadian Museums Association, 1993.

Includes only Canadian schools.

Music

Directory of Music Faculties in Colleges and Universities, U.S. and Canada, 1992-94. 14th ed. Missoula, MT: College Music Society, 1992.

Peterson's Professional Degree Programs in the Visual and Performing Arts. Princeton, NJ: Peterson's Guides, 1997.

Neurosciences

Neuroscience Training Programs in North America. Washington, DC: Association of Neuroscience Departments and Programs, 1994.

Nursing

Peterson's Guide to Nursing Programs: Baccalaureate and Graduate Nursing Education in the U.S. and Canada. 2nd ed. Princeton, NJ: Peterson's Guides, 1996.

Entrance Requirements for Nursing Education Programs in Canada/ Conditions d'admission aux programmes de formation en sciences infirmières au Canada. Ottawa, ON: Canadian Nurses Association, 1993.

Includes only Canadian schools.

Pharmacy and Pharmacology

Graduate Training in Pharmacology Programs in the United States and Canada. Bethesda, MD: American Society for Pharmacology in the United States and Canada, 1994.

Pharmacy School Admission Requirements, 1997-98. Alexandria, VA: American Association of Colleges of Pharmacy, 1996.

Includes only U.S. schools.

Resource Guide to Careers in Toxicology. 2nd ed. Reston, VA: Society of Toxicology, 1991.

Photography

The Guide to Photography Workshops & Schools. 4th ed. Coral Gables, FL: ShawGuides, 1995.

Political Science

Graduate Faculty and Programs in Political Science, 1992-1994. Spellman, Patricia, 14th ed. Washington, DC: American Political Science Association, 1992.

Planning-Urban and Regional

Guide to Graduate Education in Urban and Regional Planning. Contant, Cheryl K., Fisher, Peter S., (Editors). 10th ed. Association of Collegiate Schools of Planning, 1996.

Psychology

The Common Boundary Graduate Education Guide: Holistic Programs and Resources Integrating Spirituality and Psychology. Simpkinson, Charles H., Wengell, Douglas A., and Casavant, Mary Jane A., (Editors). 2nd ed. Bethesda, MD: Common Boundary, 1994.

Directory of Human Factors Graduate Programs in the United States and Canada. Santa Monica, CA: Human Factors Society, 1997.

Graduate Study in Psychology and Associated Fields. 28th ed. Hyattsville, MD: American Psychological Association, 1996.

Insider's Guide to Graduate Programs in Clinical Psychology, 1994/1995. Mayne, Tracy, Sayette, Michael, Norcross, John C. New York, NY: Guilford, 1994.

Graduate Guide: Description of Graduate Psychology Programmes in Canadian Universities/Répertoire des programmes d'études supérieures des départments de psychologie du Canada. 15th ed. Ottawa, ON: Canadian Psychological Association, 1996.

Includes only Canadian schools.

Social Work

Summary of Information on Master of Social Work Programs, 1994-95. Alexandria, VA: Council of Social Work Education, 1995.

Includes only U.S. schools.

CASSW Canadian Association of Schools of Social Work/ACESS Association canadienne des écoles de service social. 1995-96 ed. Ottawa, ON: Canadian Association of Schools of Social Work, 1995.

Includes only Canadian schools.

Sociology

Guide to Graduate Departments of Sociology. Albany, NY: American Sociological Association, 1997.

Teaching

Directory of Professional Programs in TESOL in the United States and Canada. Garshick, Ellen, (Editor) 1995-1997 ed. Alexandria, VA: TESOL, 1995.

Teacher Preparation: A Guide to Colleges and Universities. 1994-1995 ed. Washington, DC: National Council for Accreditation of Teacher Education, 1994.

Includes only U.S. schools.

Theatre and Dance

Dance Magazine College Guide, 1992-93: A Directory of Dance in North American Colleges and Universities. Lawson, William James, (Editor) 6th ed. New York, NY: Dance Magazine, 1992.

Veterinary Medicine

Veterinary Medical School Admission Requirements in the United States and Canada. 11th ed. Rockville, MD: Betz, 1996.

Visual Arts

Directory of M.A. and Ph.D. Programs in Art and Art History. New York, NY: College Art Association, 1995.

Directory of M.F.A. Programs in the Visual Arts. New York, NY: College Art Association, 1996.

Visual Arts Handbook. Wolff, Hennie L., (Editor) 3rd ed. Toronto, ON: Visual Arts Ontario, 1991.

Peterson's Professional Degree Programs in the Visual and Performing Arts. Princeton, NJ: Peterson's Guides, 1997.

Writing

The AWP Official Guide to Writing Programs. Fenza, D.W., and Jarock, Beth, (Editors). 7th ed. Norfolk, VA: Associated Writing Programs, 1994.

FUNDING GUIDES

Financing Graduate School: How to Get the Money You Need for Your Graduate School Education. McWade, P. (ISBN 1-56079-147-0) Peterson's Guides, 1992.

The Complete Scholarship Book. (ISBN 1-57071-127-5) Student Services, Inc., 1997.

Awards Almanac, 1996: An International Guide to Career, Research, and Education Funds. Ferrara, Miranda H., and Jaszack, Sandra, (Editors). Detroit, MI: St. James, 1995.

Profiles over 2,000 awards offered by institutions worldwide. Organized by subject and geographic area.

Athletic Scholarships: Making Your Sports Pay. Lahey, David. Toronto, ON: Warwick, 1993.

Discusses primarily U.S. athletic scholarships.

Awards for Postgraduate Study at Commonwealth Universities, 1997-99. 12th ed. London, GB: Association of Commonwealth Universities, 1997.

Lists sources of funding for graduates from one Commonwealth country to do study or research in another Commonwealth country. Has indexes by subject, place (country or city) of tenure, and by nationality/place of residence of applicant.

Awards for Study in Canada: Awards Offered to International Students and Trainees. Ottawa, ON: Canadian Bureau for International Education, 1994.

Provides a selective list of graduate awards and traineeships open to non-Canadians and tenable in Canada.

Directory of Financial Aids for Women, 1995-1997. Schlachter, Gail. San Carlos, CA: Reference Service Press, 1996.

Lists scholarships, fellowships, loans, grants, awards and internships open primarily to women. Organized by subject area and geographic region.

Directory of Scholarships, Awards and Bursaries for Post-Secondary Students with Disabilities. Ottawa, ON: National Educational Association of Disabled Students, 1993.

Educational Grants for Graduate Students Who Are Underrepresented in Higher Education: A Selected Listing of Associations, Foundations, Funds. Champaign, IL: University of Illinois at Urbana-Champaign, 1995.

Includes awards for native American Indians, Hispanics, Mexican-Americans, etc. Grants restricted to U.S. citizens or permanent residents.

Foundation Fundamentals: A Guide for Grantseekers. Nauffts, Mitchell F., (Editor) 5th ed. New York, NY: Foundation Center, 1994.

A step-by-step guide that explains the grant-seeking process. Includes a good bibliography of grant resources.

Free Money for Graduate School. Blum, Laurie. Rev. ed. New York, NY: Henry Holt, 1993.

Includes information on over 1000 grants and scholarships. Organized by subject area, with a separate index for women and one for members of ethnic minority groups.

Funding for U.S. Study: A Guide for Foreign Nationals. 2nd ed. New York, NY: Institute of International Education, 1996.

Excellent guide to funding for international students. Organized by nationality and subject area.

Worldwide Graduate Scholarship Directory. Cassidy, Daniel J. 4th ed. Franklin Lakes, NJ: Career Press, 1995.

This guide has a subject index as well as an interesting "Quick Find" index which allows access to awards by country of intended study, country of residence, ethnic background, foreign languages spoken, extracurricular activities, legal country of citizenship, religious affiliation, and more.

Grants Register, 1995-1997. 14th ed. New York, NY: St. Martin's, 1994.

Primarily intended for students at the graduate level or for those seeking further professional or advanced vocational training. The directory is international in scope and includes a subject and country index.

Peterson's Grants for Graduate & Postdoctoral Study. 4th ed. Princeton, NJ: Peterson's Guides, 1995.

This extensive guide provides access to over 1,400 fellowships, scholarships, grants, awards, and prizes.

Study Abroad/Etudes à l'étranger/Estudios en el extranjero. 29th ed. Paris: France: UNESCO, 1995.

Provides information on national and international scholarships and courses of study open to foreign students. This trilingual guide is written in English, French and Spanish and is updated every three years.

The Higher Education Moneybook for Minorities & Women: A Directory of Scholarships, Fellowships, Grants, & Loans (ISBN 0-9639490-0-4) Young, Matthews, and Cox. (To order through the publisher, phone 703-385-3065; fax 703-385-1839).

ADVISEMENT GUIDES

This section lists various guidebooks and manuals that will help prospective graduate students deal with a wide range of issues, from understanding what graduate school is all about, to tackling specific components of the application process. It is divided into two lists: The first list includes general guidebooks that deal with a variety of issues, and a the second list includes guidebooks aimed at students in particular subject areas.

General Guides

Graduate School and You: A Guide for Prospective Graduate Students. Kidwell, Clara Sue, and Lapidus, Jules B. Washington, DC: Council of Graduate Schools, 1989.

Provides a brief introduction to the process of applying to graduate school, as well as a sample timetable. Includes a section on major sources of fellowships.

The Ultimate Grad School Survival Guide: Getting In, Getting Money, Exams and Classes, the Profs, the Thesis/Dissertation. Mitchell, Lesli. Princeton, NJ: Peterson's Guides, 1996.

Over 200 pages of practical advice and tips on how to apply and succeed at graduate school. Nice format and a good annotated bibliography.

How to Get a PhD: A Handbook for Students and Their Supervisors. Phillips, Estelle M., and Pugh, D.S. 2nd ed. Buckingham, England: Open University Press, 1994.

Published in Britain, this guide provides the reader with practical, realistic information on undertaking a graduate degree. Includes information on choosing and working with a supervisor.

Graduate Student Success: The Canadian Guide. Szabo, Manfred E. Toronto, ON: Harcourt Brace Jovanovich Canada, 1995.

Discusses in depth the process of deciding to go to graduate school.

The Now Habit: A Strategic Program For Overcoming Procrastination and Enjoying Play. Fiore, N.A., J.P. Tarcher, 1989.

Eliminating Procrastination Without Putting It Off. Van Ness, R., Phi Delta Kappa Educational Foundation, 1988.

The Perfect Cover Letter. Beatty, Richard H. (ISBN 0471-50203-0) New York, NY: John Wiley & Sons, 1989.

Written for employment purposes, this handy guide describes the characteristics of good and bad cover letters as well as the basics of cover letter formats. Includes numerous sample letters.

Subject Guides

Business

How to Get into the Right Business School. Strachan, James L. Lincolnwood, IL: NTC, 1995.

Marketing Yourself to the Top Business Schools. Carpenter, Phil, and Carpenter, Carol. New York, NY: John Wiley & Sons, 1995.

Law

Getting into Law School: Strategies for the 90's. Martinson, Thomas H., and Waldherr, David P. New York, NY: Prentice-Hall, 1992.

Getting into Law School: The Canadian Guide. Johnson, Trevor V. Toronto, ON: Harcourt Brace Canada, 1996.

Guide to Law Schools in Canada. Purcell, Catherine. 1994-95 ed. Toronto, ON: ECW, 1994.

How to Get into the Right Law School. Lermack, Paul. Lincolnwood, IL: NTC, 1993.

Law School Bound: How to Get into Law School and Become a Lawyer in Canada and the U.S. Richardson, John. Oakville, ON: Richardson Press, 1992.

Medicine

Getting into Medical School: Strategies for the 90s. 2nd ed. Plantz, Scott H., Lorenzo, Nicholas Y., and Cole, Jesse A. New York, NY: Prentice Hall, 1993.

How to Get into the Right Medical School. Rogers, Carla. Lincolnwood, IL: NTC, 1996.

Medical School Admissions: The Insider's Guide. Zebala, John A., and Jones, Daniel B.   4th ed. Memphis, TN: Mustang Publishing, 1996.

Psychology

The Complete Guide to Graduate School Admission: Psychology and Related Fields.   Keith-Spiegel, Patricia. (ISBN 0-8058-0638-5) Hillsdale, NJ: Lawrence Erlbaum, 1991.

Getting In: A Step-By-Step Plan for Gaining Admission to Graduate School in Psychology.   Washington, DC: American Psychological Association, 1993 (Copies may be ordered from APA Order Dept., P.O. Box 2710, Hyattsville, MD 20784; order number 431-6340).

PERSONAL STATEMENT, ESSAY, AND INTERVIEW GUIDES

Campus Pursuit: How to Make the Most of the College Visit and Interview. Ripple, G. Gary. 4th ed. Alexandria, VA: Octameron Associates, 1991.

Graduate Admissions Essays - What Works, What Doesn't and Why. Asher, Donald. Berkeley, CA: Ten Speed Press, 1991.

Excellent guide that walks students through the admissions essay process, from formulating ideas to preparing the final draft. Includes sample essays and a section on letters of recommendation. Particularly useful for students applying into business, law or medicine.

How to Write a Winning Personal Statement for Graduate and Professional School. Stelzer, Richard J. 2nd ed. Princeton, NJ: Peterson's Guides, 1993.

Includes many sample personal statements and advice from admissions directors at several U.S. schools.

How to Write Your College Application Essay. Nourse, Kenneth A. Lincolnwood, IL: NTC, 1994.

A good basic how-to guide on application essays.

Sweaty Palms: The Neglected Art of Being Interviewed. Medley, H. Anthony. Rev. ed. Berkeley, CA: Ten Speed Press, 1992.

Written primarily with employment interviews in mind, this book nevertheless covers a wide range of topics important to those preparing for a graduate school interview. There are chapters dealing with enthusiasm, confidence, nervousness, dress, and more.

Write for Success: Preparing a Successful Professional School Application. Jackson, Evelyn W., and Bardo, Harold R. Rev. ed. Champaign, IL: National Association of Advisors for the Health Professions, 1989.

Brief guide of interest to students applying to health professions.

SPECIAL CATEGORY GUIDES

Black Student's Guide to College Success. Higgins, Ruby D., et al. Rev. ed. Westport, CT: Greenwood Press, 1994.

Excellent guide intended for undergraduate students but applicable to graduate students as well.

Directory of College Facilities and Services for People with Disabilities. Thomas, James L., and Thomas, Carol H., (Editors) 4th ed. Phoenix, AZ: Oryx, 1995.

Includes profiles of schools and their services as well as an index of disabilities served, such as: hearing impaired, speech/language impaired, brain injured etc. Coverage includes U.S. and Canada.

The Gay, Lesbian and Bisexual Students' Guide to Colleges, Universities, and Graduate Schools. Sherrill, Jan-Mitchell, and Hardesty, Craig A. New York, NY: New York University Press, 1994.

Evaluates the experiences of gay, lesbian, and bisexual students at almost 200 American colleges and universities.

The Jewish Student's Guide to American Colleges. Goldberg, Lee, and Goldberg, Lana. New York, NY: Shapolsky Publishers, 1989.

Guide intended for college-bound Jewish students. Provides lists of schools with at least 20% Jewish enrollment, schools offering kosher meals, schools with religious instruction, etc. Includes schools in U.S. and Canada.

The International Student's Guide to the American University. Barnes, Gregory A. Lincolnwood, IL: NTC, 1991.

Provides information of special interest to international students, such as arranging your visa, arriving on campus, and adjusting to graduate studies.

The Multicultural Student's Guide to Colleges: What Every African-American, Asian-American, Hispanic, and Native American Applicant Needs to Know About America's Top Schools. Mitchell, Robert. 1st ed. New York, NY: Noonday, 1993.

Includes only U.S. schools.

The Resource Directory of Disabled Student Services at Canadian Universities and Colleges. Ottawa, ON: National Association of Disabled Students, 1993.

Describes services for disabled students at 136 universities and colleges across Canada. Lists people to contact at each institution.

Peterson's Colleges with Programs for Students with Learning Disabilities. 3rd ed. Mangrum, Charles T., and Strichart, Stephen S. Princeton, NJ: Peterson's Guides, 1992.

Provides advice for learning-disabled students as well as profiles on services available at several U.S. schools.

Successfully Negotiating the Graduate School Process: A Guide for Minority Students. Adams, Howard G. Rev. ed. Notre Dame, IN: National Consortium for Graduate Degrees for Minorities in Engineering and Science, 1990.

Designed to encourage minorities to consider graduate school. Includes information on funding and a good glossary of terms.

Women's Colleges. Adler, Joe Anne, and Friedman, Jennifer Adler. New York, NY: Prentice Hall, 1994.

Provides profiles of over 75 women's colleges in the United States.

INTERNET SITES

The Internet can be a great way to explore graduate schools. And one can do it all from the comfort of home!

To begin with, most universities now have home pages where potential applicants can access a school's academic calendar and admission information. Also, there are many good sites that allow searching of universities by program and/or which provide information on rankings of schools and sources of funding.

Here is a list of just a few selected sites to get you started. It is certainly not comprehensive as new sites are being established every day, and many are changing their addresses. It is recommended that you use electronic sources in combination with printed directories in order to ensure as complete topic coverage as possible. Do not rely on just one source for your information.

College Board

http://www.collegeboard.org/

Using "college search" one can access U.S. programs by subject, geographic area, or level of program (undergraduate, graduate etc.).

Emory Colossal List of Career Links

http://www.emory.edu/CAREER/Links.html

As well as providing job search information, this site also includes access to graduate and professional schools. Allows searching of schools by program and provides links to many related sites.

Graduate School Guide
http://www.schoolguides.com/

Guide to doctoral, master's and professional degree programs. Provides school profiles and allows searching by field of study.

Peterson's Education and Career Centre

http://www.petersons.com/

Includes information on graduate study, studying abroad, financing your education, distance learning and much more. Contains references to U.S. and Canadian schools.

U.S. News Online.EDU: Colleges and Careers Center

http://www.usnews.com/usnews/edu/?/home.htm

Provides information on choosing a graduate school, including the "1997 Graduate School Rankings." It also links to useful financial aid sites.

Yahoo's Graduate School Directory

http://www.wlu.edu/~career/yahoo.html

Includes information on medical, business and law schools. Content is primarily American with selected international schools.

The Association of Neuroscience Departments and Programs

http://www.andp.org/training

A comprehensive listing and description of graduate neuroscience programs in the United States, Canada and Mexico. It also provides tips on how to apply and what to look for in a neuroscience program.

The Council of Graduate Schools (CGS)

http://www.cgsnet.org

Lots of information and guidance for current and prospective graduate students, including advisement guides and other publications that can be ordered on-line. This site also has a section aimed at issues of interest to graduate faculty and administrators, and thus provides students with an opportunity to "watch and listen" as these important decision-makers express their views concerning graduate education.

Index

Readers should note that the *Resources* section is not included in this index. Like any book index, this one is meant to help the reader navigate to important information in the book. The Resources section should be used as a separate index — one that will help its users navigate to useful information in places other than this book.

To order copies of this book:

Write to

Proto Press
Order Dept., P.O. Box 818
Hudson, Quebec
Canada J0P 1H0

Indicate the name of the book you wish to purchase and the quantity and enclose a check for $19.95 U.S. per book ($24.95 Canada; Quebec residents add $1.75 per book), plus $2.00 shipping for the first book and 75 cents for each additional book. Surface shipping may take three to four weeks; the air mail shipping rate is $3.50 per book.